First Steps in the SAP® Purchasing Processes (MM)

2nd, extended edition

Claudia Jost

Thank you for purchasing this book from Espresso Tutorials!

Like a cup of espresso coffee, Espresso Tutorials SAP books are concise and effective. We know that your time is valuable and we deliver information in a succinct and straightforward manner. It only takes our readers a short amount of time to consume SAP concepts. Our books are well recognized in the industry for leveraging tutorial-style instruction and videos to show you step by step how to successfully work with SAP.

Check out our YouTube channel to watch our videos at
https://www.youtube.com/user/EspressoTutorials.

If you are interested in SAP Finance and Controlling, join us at
http://www.fico-forum.com/forum2/
to get your SAP questions answered and contribute to discussions.

Related titles from Espresso Tutorials:

▶ Björn Weber: First Steps in the SAP® Production Processes (PP)
  http://5027.espresso-tutorials.com

▶ Stephen Birchall: Invoice Verification for SAP®
  http://5073.espresso-tutorials.com

▶ Uwe Göhring: Capacity Planning with SAP®
  http://5080.espresso-tutorials.com

▶ Avijt Dutta & Shreekant Shiralkar: Demand Planning with SAP® APO—Concepts and Design
  http://5105.espresso-tutorials.com

▶ Avijt Dutta & Shreekant Shiralkar: Demand Planning with SAP® APO—Execution
  http://5106.espresso-tutorials.com

▶ Tobias Götz, Anette Götz: Practical Guide to SAP® Transportation Management (2nd edition)
  http://5082.espresso-tutorials.com

▶ Matthew Johnson: SAP® Material Master—A Practical Guide, 2nd edition
  http://5190.espresso-tutorials.com

▶ Sydnie McConnell & Martin Munzel: First Steps in SAP®, 2nd extended edition: *http://5045.espresso-tutorials.com*

Claudia Jost
First Steps in SAP® Purchasing Processes (MM), 2nd, extended edition

ISBN:	978-1-5482-2713-5
Editor:	Anja Achilles
Translation:	Tracey Duffy
Proofreading:	Lisa Jackson
Cover Design:	Philip Esch
Cover Photo:	fotolia #112860856 zeber
Interior Design:	Johann-Christian Hanke

All rights reserved.

2nd Edition 2017, Gleichen

© 2017 by Espresso Tutorials GmbH

URL: *www.espresso-tutorials.com*

Feedback
We greatly appreciate any feedback you may have concerning this book. Please send your feedback via email to: *info@espresso-tutorials.com*.

Table of Contents

Foreword

Nearly 80% of Fortune 500 companies use the SAP ERP (Enterprise Resource Planning) software to plan and deploy their resources optimally.

Almost all of these companies use the SAP modules FI and CO for their financial processes. Many of them have also been using the SAP module *Materials Management* to manage their materials for a long time. Regardless of whether you are just starting out in procurement or are a student of the subject, in this tutorial I will explain the Materials Management module of the SAP system from the view of a user. The information provided should enable you to perform the main operational process in the module on your own.

The tutorial does not present all of the options that this module offers comprehensively—it describes a selection of the frequently used functions in a complete procurement process, from setting up a purchase requisition to posting the vendor invoice. It also gives you tips for improving processes and to make your work easier. My explanations focus on the fact that the procurement process can be executed in the standard SAP system without any errors. An excursus provides information about master data that may be helpful—such as the material master and the purchasing info record—because in principle, you can set up and settle a purchase order without creating this basic data. However, you will still find various information and tips that go beyond the standard application. These make daily use of the SAP system more comfortable and improve the quality of the process.

Acknowledgments

First and foremost, my thanks go to Mr. Martin Munzel at Espresso Tutorials for giving me the opportunity to document my experiences with the SAP system in a book. Thanks also to his wife, Mrs. Renata Munzel, who set up the initial contact.

I would also like to thank Ms. Anja Achilles who proofread the original German version of the book and gave it the finishing touch.

Heartfelt thanks go to "my trusted system administrator," who guided me through the technology and constantly encouraged me to be inquisitive.

And of course, special thanks also to my family—they support me in daily life and in my projects and give me the freedom I need to do my work.

We have added a few icons to highlight important information. These include:

Tips
Tips highlight information that provides more details about the subject being described and/or additional background information.

Examples
Examples help illustrate a topic better by relating it to real world scenarios.

Attention
Attention notices highlight information that you should be aware of when you go through the examples in this book on your own.

Finally, a note concerning the copyright: all screenshots printed in this book are the copyright of SAP SE. All rights are reserved by SAP SE. Copyright pertains to all SAP images in this publication. For the sake of simplicity, we do not mention this specifically underneath every screenshot.

1 Introduction to the SAP Materials Management (MM) module

The aim of this tutorial is to give you an initial overview of the SAP module Materials Management (MM). It will enable you to execute the main operative process in the MM module independently.

The tasks of materials management are described in the six Rs:

- ▶ The right goods
- ▶ In the right quantity
- ▶ At the right price
- ▶ At the right time
- ▶ In the right quality
- ▶ At the right place

Materials management includes the following main functions:

- ▶ *Purchasing:* defines the source of supply, allowing a purchase requisition or purchase order to be set up. It also includes the controlling for the ordering process (order acknowledgments, deliveries, etc.).
- ▶ Goods receipts and reservations are posted in *warehouse management and inventory management.*
- ▶ In *incoming invoice verification,* supplier invoices are recorded and the details of the invoices are checked against the details in the purchase orders, e. g., prices or payment targets. Provided there are no differences, the invoice is released for payment.
- ▶ In the *valuation* area, material price changes are implemented for the balance sheet valuation and actual costing.
- ▶ *Material counts* is the recording of physical inventory documents, and, where applicable, difference postings take place in the *inventory* cluster.

In this tutorial, you will encounter various terms for the assignment of business transactions to business areas, projects, products, etc. The connections and relationships between company units depend on the structure of the company (defined in customizing) and therefore, they cannot be explained in terms that are valid generally. However, the most important organizational terms are explained briefly below.

- ▶ Client: highest level organizational unit; an independent unit for the purposes of commercial law, organization, and data technology.

- ▶ Company code: generally used for the smallest self-contained legal unit.

- ▶ Plant: unit that structures the company from the planning, procurement, and production perspectives. Within a company, one plant can be a supplier for another plant—a service unit, for example.

- ▶ Purchasing organization: the unit within Logistics which executes the purchasing processes.

- ▶ Storage location: organizational unit for differentiating between company units in which materials are stored. The responsibility for inventory can also be differentiated based on storage locations (e. g., plant inventory vs. supplier inventory).

- ▶ Purchasing group: persons or groups of persons who, within the procurement organization, are responsible for defined product groups, suppliers, or processes.

Due to the company-specific customizing settings, there may be slight deviations to your system.

2 The main process in SAP MM

In this chapter, I guide you through the procurement process step by step so that you can follow the process in your own system.

The high proportion of companies that use the MM module is an indicator of the special significance that goods management has within a company. It also underlines the importance of well-organized materials management as a condition for business success. Targeted planning and control of the flows of materials, as well as regular determination of requirements and requirement fulfillment, are important success factors, particularly in markets that demand high flexibility with low levels of storage. Customers require 100% ability to deliver and adhere to delivery schedules.

Using an SAP system to process purchase orders means that you can no longer post invoices without a reference to a purchase order. In large companies in particular, this is an important factor in ensuring that invoices are correct. It is also important for ensuring the transparency provided by a dual control principle which has to be observed and which is also required by auditing companies.

An additional requirement that the ERP system must fulfill is transparency over the stocks available, storage retention periods, and future availability of goods and services.

This tutorial is restricted to the main procurement process in the MM area—a process that is also used by companies that do not have a complex supply chain organization. Figure 2.1 shows this main process in a standardized form.

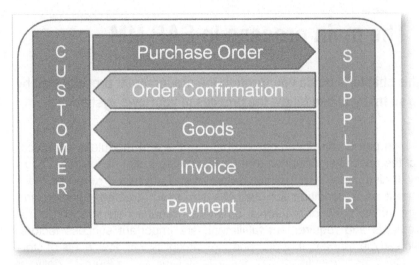

Figure 2.1: General representation of the procurement process

The main process is:

▶ Create a vendor master record

▶ Create a purchase requisition

▶ Convert the purchase requisition into a purchase order

▶ Post the goods receipt

▶ Post the vendor invoice

Creating favorites

 You can search for transactions via the menu tree or enter the transaction code directly. For your daily work, it is advisable to define frequently used transactions as favorites. You can manage these like in Windows Explorer by creating folders (see Section 4.4).

In general, we can say that as the quality (= completeness and accuracy) of the data increases in the SAP system, the quality of the processes also increases. At the same time, the time required to complete processes falls because there are fewer or, in an ideal situation, no queries or questions.

2.1 General guide for using the SAP system

Before we look at the *purchase order* business process, I will explain some of the icons you will encounter frequently in the SAP system.

By clicking the green checkmark ✅ , you can confirm your entries. If any entries are missing from or are incorrect in the form you are processing, the system then shows these entries. If all of the entries are complete and correct, no further message appears and you can save the document.

By clicking the 🖫 icon, you can save the final purchase orders, for example. Once you have clicked this icon when creating a purchase order, the system creates the purchase order and a message containing the *purchase order number* appears at the bottom of the screen.

Before you save your entries by clicking ✅ , you can check them. Click 🔊 to display all messages relating to an item. The (warning) bell icon 🔔 indicates whether there are any messages for the item in question. The 🔔 icon may be displayed as an alternative to the warning bell.

Using the expand 🔲 and collapse 🗁 icons, you can display detailed information or, to make a screen clearer and easier to read, hide detailed information.

Within a transaction, you can use the 🖉 icon to switch from display to change mode or vice versa.

To create a new document, click ☐ .

You can use the garbage can icon 🗑 to remove items from purchase requisitions. To do this, select the relevant item and then click the icon.

The traffic light color indicates the current processing status of the document—a purchase order, for example:

🔴⚪⚪ A red traffic light indicates that some required data is still missing from the document. Double-click the traffic light icon to show which entry or entries is/are missing. In a purchase order, this could be the delivery date, delivery quantity, or an account assignment. You cannot save and thus create the purchase order if this data is missing.

⊙⊙⊙ A yellow traffic light indicates a warning. It appears, for example, if the delivery date you have entered is not the same as the calculated delivery date, or the price you have entered does not match the price defined in the system. You can still save the purchase order in this status.

⊙⊙⊙ A green traffic light indicates that all required information is present and there are no deviations from the basic data defined in the system, from the info record, or from the material master. You can save the purchase order.

By clicking 🔄 you can start an evaluation, such as the list display of the purchase orders.

In an SAP system, you can open up to eight sessions in parallel. A *session* is a processing window. If you want to execute multiple tasks in different SAP functions, open multiple sessions. This allows you, for example, to create a purchase order in one session and call up the list displays for the purchasing info records in another session. This makes your work easier because you only have to switch between windows and you do not have to end any processing steps first.

To create database entries in an SAP system, you use a transaction. In general SAP terminology usage, a *transaction* can also be used to refer to an evaluation. The *transaction code* is the character string that you use to call up a function in an SAP system. Within a transaction click the 🔲 icon to open a new session.

Working in multiple sessions

 If you are processing a purchase order or a material number with multiple sessions in parallel, you must have completed one session by saving; otherwise, the material or the purchase order is blocked for processing. This is due to the database logic used in SAP systems.

2.2 Creating a vendor master record

In the SAP system, you need a vendor master record in order to assign business transactions to an account. The vendor master record can be temporary; this is useful if you expect only one business transaction for the vendor, for example. In this case, you create a one-time vendor. This enables you to reduce the number of vendor master records in the system. If you expect multiple business transactions for a vendor, you can set up a permanent vendor master record.

The vendor master record consists of the following parts:

▶ A purchasing part (created with transaction MK01): contains all of the data required to set up a purchase order

▶ An accounting part (created with transaction FK01): contains all of the data required to process the payment

The purchasing view is generally created by the procurement department in order to place the purchase order with a new vendor. The accounting view is usually created by the accounting department as soon as the vendor invoice with the required data is available. One of the reasons for this is segregation of duties (SoD); it is also required to satisfy audit requirements.

Using templates

 You can create vendors for similar or identical product groups by using an existing vendor as a template. In addition to making the task easier, this also ensures that agreed standards are maintained for each product group.

2.2.1 Creating the purchasing view

In the purchasing view, you assign an SAP account to the vendor. Business transactions are then posted to this account. The data from the vendor master is also transferred to the purchase requisition or purchase order as default values (e. g., payment targets, Incoterms).

You access this view via the following menu path: SAP MENU • LOGISTICS • MATERIALS MANAGEMENT • PURCHASING • MASTER DATA • VENDOR • PUR- CHASING • CREATE (see Figure 2.2. Alternatively, you can enter transac- tion code MK01 (see Figure 2.3).

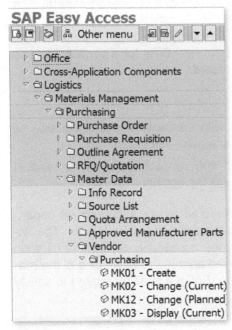

Figure 2.2: Creating a vendor: purchasing

Figure 2.3: Creating a vendor: entering the transaction code

Once you have called up transaction MK01, the view shown in Figure 2.4 appears.

The access for creating a vendor master record depends on the system settings. In this example, I will show you how to create a vendor. The vendor number is assigned externally, which means that you have to enter the number when you create the vendor master record.

You have to enter the first details: the assignment of a vendor number (field: VENDOR) and the entry of the PURCHASING ORGANIZATION are mandatory fields—no further processing is possible if these entries are missing.

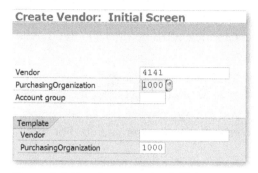

Create Vendor: Initial Screen

Vendor	4141
PurchasingOrganization	1000
Account group	

Template	
Vendor	
PurchasingOrganization	1000

Figure 2.4: Creating a vendor: initial screen

Alternatively, you can use the account group instead of the purchasing organization—for the vendor in our example, this is **KRED**. The *account group* is a group of vendors in which the same criteria apply to all vendors within the group. For example, these vendors all supply to a defined purchasing organization or plant.

You start the creation of the vendor master record (see Figure 2.5) by pressing **Enter**.

⊞ ⊞ ⊞ MENA Certificate

Search Terms					
Search term 1/2	WINDE				

Street Address					
Street/House number	Windmühlenstr.		17		
Postal Code/City	12345	Mühldorf			
Country	DE	Germany	Region	05	Nrth Rhine Westfalia

PO Box Address	
PO Box	
Postal code	

Communication					
Language	German			Other communication...	
Telephone	123 456	Extension	789		
Fax	123 456	Extension	987		
E-Mail	g.winde@gewinde.de				
Data line					
Telebox					

Figure 2.5: Creating a vendor: address

The example above shows the fields that require entries for problem-free process management. In particular, here you should select a useful SEARCH TERM that enables other users to find this vendor in the system. This avoids the situation where your colleagues create a duplicate entry for this vendor in the system because they could not find it in the master data.

Standardizing the vendor names used

I recommend that you define conventions for assigning vendor names in order to simplify the search. For example:

▶ No abbreviations

▶ Upper case only

▶ No first names

On the next screen (see Figure 2.6), you have to enter the tax data:

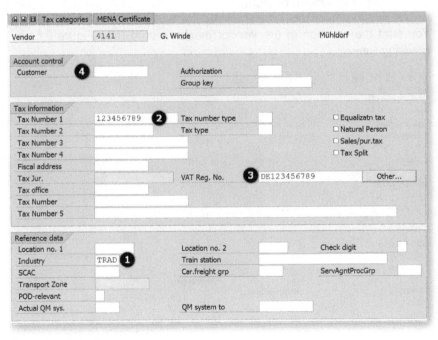

Figure 2.6: Creating a vendor: tax

In the TAX view, you can assign the vendor to an INDUSTRY ❶ and define the TAX NUMBER ❷ and the SALES TAX NUMBER (also known as the VAT registration number) ❸. If the vendor is also a customer in your company, you can enter the number of the customer master record in the CUSTOMER ❹ field.

In the window that opens (see Figure 2.7), you assign the parameters that are filled as default values whenever the vendor is accessed in the future.

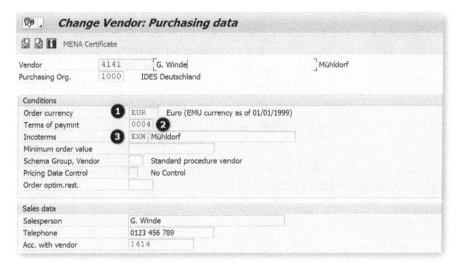

Figure 2.7: Creating a vendor: purchasing data (1)

In addition to the contact data, the purchasing conditions such as ORDER CURRENCY ❶, TERMS OF PAYMENT ❷, and INCOTERMS ❸ are particularly important here.

▶ Order currency = the currency in which you place orders with the vendor. If the order currency is not the same as the local currency, an exchange rate defined in the SAP system is used to determine the release limits (see also Section 2.4.1 for more information about the release procedure).

▶ Terms of payment = definition of the period within which the vendor invoice is paid. You can also define cash discount agreements here, for example.

▶ Incoterms = definition of the type and means of delivery and the transfer of risks, as well as the definition of which business partner bears the transport and insurance costs. The Incoterms rules were first issued by the International Chamber of Commerce in 1936, with the latest revision in January 2011 (Incoterms 2010).

This information is used to set up purchase requisitions and purchase orders automatically.

Entering Incoterms

It is extremely important for the person ordering materials or creating a purchase order to know how to handle Incoterms. The law of obligations applies here, and issues regarding insurance, transport costs, and payment of customs duty are defined. In the event of a claim, the company can incur significant (financial) expense.

Further purchasing data is required to standardize the process between your company and the vendor (see Figure 2.8).

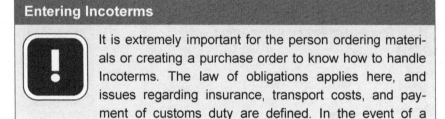

Figure 2.8: Creating a vendor: purchasing data (2)

The goods receipt-based invoice verification is particularly worthy of mention here ❶ (field: GR-BASED INV. VERIF.). If this option is selected, an incoming invoice is checked against a goods receipt; an invoice is only released for payment if the delivery or service corresponds to what the vendor has invoiced. The entry of a duty of acknowledgment ❷ can also contribute to process security. If there is no order acknowledgment within the periods defined by the CONFIRMATION CONTROL ❸, the system issues a reminder.

Further entries simplify the setting up of purchase requisitions or purchase orders.

This completes the creation of the vendor master record and you can save it by clicking 💾. The following message appears in the footer:

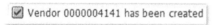

Vendor 0000004141 has been created

Process security through the use of control data

If you use the control data consistently (e. g., the GR-BASED INV. VERIF. or ACKNOWLEDGMENT REQD checkboxes), this defines the default settings in the purchase orders and has a positive effect on the procurement process: invoices can be posted against the goods receipt and do not have to be released separately. You can configure warning messages for situations where order acknowledgments are outstanding; the messages indicate a possible problem in the transmission of the purchase order. This allows you to speed up the invoice process and supports security of supplies.

2.2.2   Creating the accounting view

When you create the accounting view, the SAP system automatically assigns line item display and open item management to the vendor. The accounting view also contains all relevant information for processing the payment automatically.

The creation of the accounting view is a transaction in the FI area. This segregation of duties ensures a clear separation between the individual areas of responsibility. I will not address the creation of the FI master data in this tutorial.

2.2.3 Useful entries and settings

On the initial screen of the vendor master, you define the communication data for the vendor (see Figure 2.9).

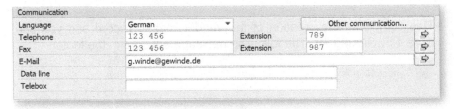

Figure 2.9: Vendor master: communication data

Click ⇨ to open a second window where you can define additional contact information (see Figure 2.10).

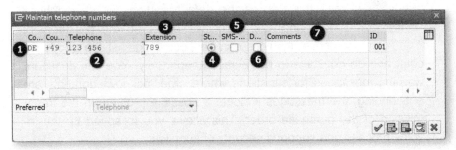

Figure 2.10: Vendor master record: adding communication data

Click 🔲 to activate a further line in which, as shown in this example, you can add a telephone number. Note the following:

❶ The international area code is defined by the country code. You do not have to enter any numbers here.

❷ Under TELEPHONE, enter the telephone number without the leading zero for the area code.

❸ Under EXTENSION, enter the extension number.

❹ Using this field, you can define whether the contact is a standard contact. This is then the default entry in all fields in which the telephone number of the vendor is displayed.

❺ This field defines whether the telephone number can be used for SMS messages.

❻ Here you can note that this number is not used for automatic communication from the SAP system. This is particularly important for fax numbers and e-mail addresses.

❼ Under COMMENTS, you can enter additional information—for example, for colleagues who also work with the vendor. Your colleagues can then see, for instance, which area the respective contact works in (see Figure 2.11).

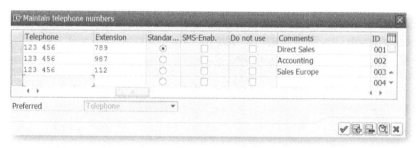

Figure 2.11: Vendor master: example of communication data

You can also create further communication data for the fax number and e-mail addresses in the same way.

Vendor master data

There will always be some colleagues who delete information in the vendor master or change the parameters you have configured. To prevent this, it can be helpful to enter your own telephone number in the comments (e. g., your extension). If you are lucky, colleagues will take the opportunity to ask questions before making any changes.

2.3 Creating a purchase requisition

The *purchase requisition* is not a purchase order to a vendor; it is an internal request from a specific department to the purchasing department to procure a service or a material in a specific quantity for a specific date.

The purchase requisition can be subject to a release process. In addition to the creation of the actual requisition note by the requisitioner, this process then ensures that the cost center manager is informed and approves the procurement.

You can access the transaction via the following menu path: SAP MENU • LOGISTICS • MATERIALS MANAGEMENT • PURCHASING • PURCHASE REQUISITION • CREATE. Alternatively, you can enter transaction code ME51N directly.

Figure 2.12 shows the structure of a purchase requisition. It consists of a header section, an item section, and the item details. You will also see this structure in the purchase orders.

The header section contains all of the information required for the items in a purchase order:

▶ Vendor

▶ Payment terms

▶ Incoterms

▶ Person creating the purchase order/contact person

The header is valid for the complete purchase order purchase requisition. So if you have different payment terms for different line items you have to issue a new order.

The item section contains all of the specific information about a product, material, or service, for example:

▶ Price, price unit, currency

▶ Delivery date or schedule line

▶ Delivery address

▶ Because each material has an item section, you can enter different values for each item of information shown above. e. g., if you

want the goods to go to different locations, you only need to issue one purchase requisition.

> **Purchase requisitions with schedule lines**
>
> If, instead of creating individual requisitions for each
> requirement, you create purchase requisitions with
> schedule lines, you give the buyer the opportunity to
> achieve a better price due to a higher quantity. At the
> same time, the vendor can optimize their own process-
> es, for example by bundling production batches. Furthermore, there is
> no unnecessary debit to the warehouse stock, either in terms of value
> or volume.

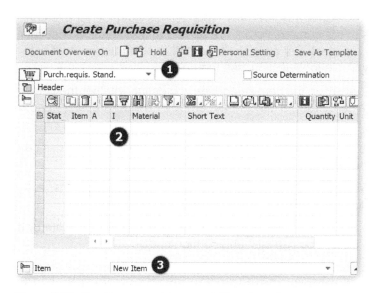

Figure 2.12: Creating a purchase requisition: layout

❶ In the header section, you can define general information for the
purchase requisition in an internal header memo in the form of text
with automatic word wraparound.

❷ In the items section, you define the specific data for the service or
the material (see also Figure 2.13).

27

❸ In the item details, you can then enter additional information for the purchase order item (see Figure 2.13).

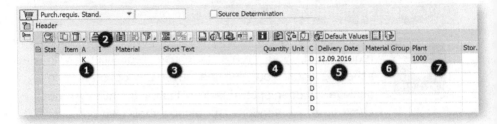

Figure 2.13: Creating a purchase requisition: item 1

Initially, you should enter all of the general information for the purchase order, as shown in Figure 2.15 . This includes:

❶ ACCOUNT ASSIGNMENT CATEGORY: This defines whether, for example, the costs of the purchase order are posted to a material, a cost center, or to a project. For an overview of the account assignment categories available for selection, see Figure 2.14.

❷ ITEM CATEGORY: In the item categories you define whether the item is a consignment order, a subcontract order, or a stock transfer, for example.

❸ MATERIAL or SHORT TEXT: Here, the person placing the order can specify the service or material to be procured.

❹ QUANTITY/UNIT: The quantity can be entered in various units, e. g., piece or kilo.

❺ DELIVERY DATE: You can enter the delivery date as a fixed date or a calendar week. You can also enter a month.

❻ MATERIAL GROUP: The material group assigns the purchase order to various material fields internally.

❼ PLANT: By specifying the plant, you define the organizational, and thus accounting, assignment for the purchase order.

Further data can be added but is not mandatory. Different companies will have different requirements.

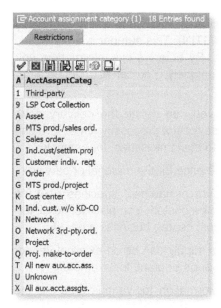

Figure 2.14: Creating a purchase requisition: selecting the account assignment category

Figure 2.15 shows an example of the help function that the system offers for filling the individual fields. By clicking the icon to the right of a field, you can display a selection list that contains SAP standard values (as well as company-specific values where applicable). You can enter information in all relevant fields in this way.

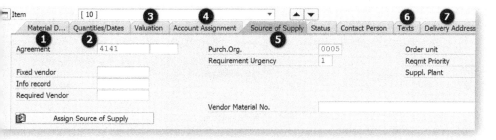

Figure 2.15: Creating a purchase requisition: item details

To process a purchase requisition quickly and without any problems, you should also enter all known information for the item details (see Figure 2.15). This concerns the following areas:

❶ MATERIAL DATA: Here you can define an EAN code or the commonly used Global Trade Item Number (GTIN). This number is a distinctive international code for trade items. By entering this information, you specify the goods to be procured uniquely. You can also define a delivery batch.

❷ QUANTITIES/DATES: On this tab, you can define the delivery date, planned delivery time, and a goods receipt processing time. You can use it to define waiting times due to customs issues, for example.

❸ VALUATION: Here you can enter the price for the material or service.

❹ ACCOUNT ASSIGNMENT: The account assignment specifies how the costs of the purchase order are to be posted. You also define all further details for the posting, e. g., cost center, business area, etc.

❺ SOURCE OF SUPPLY: The source of supply can be an external vendor or another area of the company—another plant, for example.

❻ TEXTS: You can define further information for various areas of the purchase order. This can be a material purchase order text or a delivery text, for example.

❼ DELIVERY ADDRESS: You can specify the recipient and the exact address for the goods or services here.

Value lists for entering information in the fields are also offered here.

In this example, on the SOURCE OF SUPPLY tab (see Figure 2.16), we have named the vendor we created in Section 2.2.

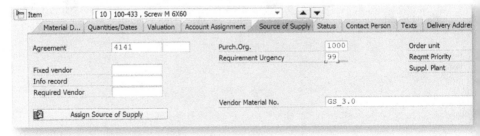

Figure 2.16: Creating a purchase requisition: item details, source of supply

Once you have defined all of the known data, press **Enter** to check whether there is an entry in every required field. If this is not the case, an error indicator appears in the STATUS column, as shown in Figure 2.17.

Figure 2.17: Creating a purchase requisition: item status

By double-clicking the red traffic light, you can display specific information about missing entries for the item concerned (see Figure 2.18).

Figure 2.18: Creating a purchase requisition: item status details

If you enter a checkmark in the white box and confirm by pressing the **Enter** key or clicking the green checkmark at the bottom left, the system takes you to the fields that require entries.

You can then save the purchase requisition by clicking 🔲. Once you have saved, the purchase requisition number appears in the footer:

☑ Purchase requisition number 0010029492 created

Information in the purchase requisition

 In line with the saying, "information only harms those who do not have it," in my opinion, the person requesting goods and services should enter all known information in the purchase requisition. Even if time is often in short supply in everyday business, a purchase requisition that has been filled out carefully prevents queries from the purchasing department or from vendors. This saves time for everybody involved and the goods can be delivered more quickly.

2.4 Converting the purchase requisition

The purchase order is the document that is sent to the external business partner, usually by the purchasing department.

Before the purchase requisition can be processed further, it has to be released by a specific department and/or cost center controlling.

2.4.1 Releasing the purchase requisition

The purchase requisition is generally released by the cost center manager. This enables him to get an overview of whether the budget is being adhered to and at the same time, he can decide whether a purchase requisition is to be implemented or not.

For the release in the SAP system, you can also define a release strategy. This strategy defines the persons who have to release a purchase requisition and the order in which they have to do so. The release can refer to a complete purchase requisition, although individual purchase requisition items can be converted into purchase order items as well.

In theory, a purchase requisition can be converted without being released; however, this is not usually done in practice.

If you follow the path LOGISTICS • MATERIALS MANAGEMENT • PURCHASING • PURCHASE REQUISITION • RELEASE • INDIVIDUAL RELEASE, the view shown in Figure 2.19 appears:

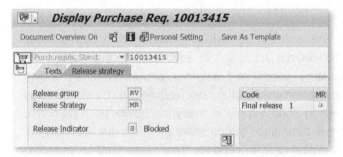

Figure 2.19: Releasing the purchase requisition: overview

You release the purchase requisition by clicking , and it can now be converted into a purchase order.

2.4.2   Creating a purchase order

In this process, from the internal requirement, you create a purchase order that is sent to the external business partner.

Follow the path SAP MENU • LOGISTICS • MATERIALS MANAGEMENT • PURCHASING • PURCHASE ORDER • CREATE • VENDOR/SUPPLYING PLANT KNOWN to display the CREATE PURCHASE ORDER view shown in Figure 2.20:

St	Itm	A	I	Material	Short Text	PO Quantity	OUn	C	Deliv. Date	Net Price	Curren

Create Purchase Order

Document Overview On   □ ♂ Hold ⚅ ⚅ Print Preview   Messages 🄸 ⚅ Personal Setting   Save As Template   Load from Template

Standard PO   Vendor   Doc. date   21.08.2016

Figure 2.20: Creating a purchase order: item

Alternatively, you can call up transaction ME21N directly.

To call up the purchase requisition that you have created, you have to select it in the DOCUMENT OVERVIEW (see Figure 2.21). You can define in advance which document type, for example purchase orders, contracts, or requests for quotation, should be displayed.

Figure 2.21: Converting a purchase requisition: document overview, selection of document type

In the document overview, you can either select items from the purchase requisition or convert the entire purchase requisition into a purchase order. You can transfer the items to the purchase order by selecting the COPY icon  (see Figure 2.22).

Figure 2.22: Converting a purchase requisition: selecting items

Searching for documents

You can also use the document overview to search for further documents—for example, your own purchase orders or held purchase orders. The overview also contains scheduling agreements or queries.

The example in Figure 2.23 indicates an error message again. Here too you can double-click the yellow traffic light △ to query and process the error message.

Figure 2.23: Converting a purchase requisition: error status

The error message shows that the delivery date is in the past (see Figure 2.24).

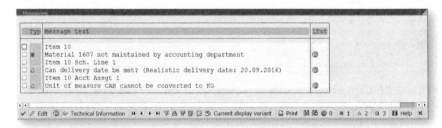

Figure 2.24: Converting a purchase requisition: error message details

However, the yellow traffic light also means that these errors are not critical and you can still save the purchase order. You confirm the error message by pressing the Enter key or clicking the green checkmark ✔. Once you have saved the purchase order 💾, a purchase order number is assigned:

> ☑ Standard PO created under the number 4500024049

If, when creating a purchase order, you do not have all of the relevant data or this data has not been defined in the SAP system, you can close the purchase order by *holding* it. As soon as all of the required parameters have been configured in the system and all required information is available, you can call up this held purchase order using transaction ME21N (CREATE PURCHASE ORDER) and then process and save it.

2.5   Recording goods receipt

By law, commercial businesses are obliged to document goods receipts. This applies for all goods, irrespective of whether they are intended for resale or consumption. From a process perspective, by posting the goods receipt, you document the fact that goods or services ordered have been delivered or provided. Within the purchase order, this is visible in the *purchase order history*. A prerequisite for the goods receipt posting may be that a shipping notification has been posted to the purchase order item beforehand.

From an organizational perspective, inventory management does not generally belong to the area of responsibility of procurement or purchasing. For audit purposes, the area that sets up the purchase order must be separate from the area that posts the goods receipt to ensure the principle of *segregation of duties (SoD)*. For all companies listed on the stock exchange, every year there is a review of the SAP authorizations granted to all employees in order to avoid abuse of authorizations.

The aim of the real-time posting of goods receipts and goods issues is to ensure that the actual stocks available are shown in the SAP system. This is also important for the financial statements for which, amongst other things, the stock figures are used to evaluate the asset items.

However, although the goods receipt posting is not strictly within the scope of this tutorial, I will outline this process step briefly to give you a better overview of the overall process.

2.5.1   Entering a shipping notification

A *shipping notification* is the notification of an inward goods movement and it is sent by the vendor. This document confirms that the goods have been produced and packaged. A delivery note has also been created and the handover to the carrier is therefore imminent. The shipping notification is therefore more than an order acknowledgment in which the vendor merely confirms the conditions of the purchase order, such as the price, payment target, and Incoterms, without the product necessarily being finished. The probability that the materials will be delivered promptly is therefore greater.

A shipping notification is also displayed in the stock and requirements overview (transaction MD04). If you configure the customizing such that these shipping notifications are taken into account in materials planning, your production planning is also more transparent.

Shipping notification

For deliveries from Asia, which are usually at sea for several weeks, the shipping notification is a good opportunity to get an overview of the materials that will soon be arriving.

Follow the path SAP MENU • LOGISTICS • MATERIALS MANAGEMENT • PURCHASING • PURCHASE ORDER • CHANGE or use transaction code ME22N directly to open the purchase order view (see Figure 2.25).

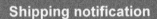

Held Standard PO 4500017296 Created by Claudia (Espresso Tutoria											
Document Overview On			Print Preview	Messages	Personal Setting	Save As Template	Load from Template				
Standard PO		4500017296	Vendor		4141 G. Winde			Doc. date	21.08.2016		
Header											
St	Itm	A I	Material	Short Text		PO Quantity	OUn	C Deliv. Date	Net Price		Curr
	10	K	1607	1607 screw		50	CAR	D 12.10.2016	1,50		EUR

Figure 2.25: Entering a shipping notification purchase order view

The system shows the last purchase order that you saved or called up. Since in most cases, this is not the purchase order for which you wish to enter a shipping notification, you have to select the correct purchase order by clicking OTHER DOCUMENT 🔁 (see Figure 2.26).

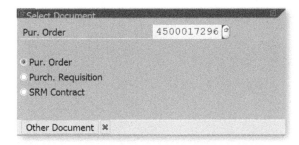

Figure 2.26: Entering a shipping notification: other purchase order

In the text field that opens, you can now enter the number of the purchase order for which you want to create a shipping notification. Confirm by selecting OTHER DOCUMENT or by pressing **Enter**.

Documents from vendors

Your vendor should be obliged to send all relevant data with an order acknowledgment or a shipping notification. This avoids any unnecessary effort which would be involved in searching for a purchase order number, for example. The document should contain the following information:

▶ Purchase order number

▶ Material number

▶ Delivery date

▶ Price and price unit

▶ Vendor's material number

▶ Payment terms

▶ Incoterm

The purchase order that you selected is displayed, and in the item details, you can click the CONFIRMATIONS tab. Alternatively, to the right of the item details, you can click 🔲 to access the list shown in Figure 2.27. Click a term to open the corresponding tab.

Material Data
Quantities/Weights
Delivery Schedule
Delivery
Invoice
Conditions
Account Assignment
Texts
Delivery Address
ⱽ Confirmations
Condition Control
Retail

Figure 2.27: Entering a shipping notification, confirmations

The confirmation category (CC) is particularly important here. Confirmation category AB indicates an order acknowledgment. In a normal situation, this is expected shortly after the purchase order is sent. It states that the vendor has received the purchase order and has scheduled pre-material procurement, production, and delivery such that he will deliver the materials for the date specified in the order acknowledgment.

The shipping notification confirmation category (**LA**) is more stringent than the order acknowledgment, meaning that the probability that the goods will be delivered at the specified time is greater. In this case, the vendor has already produced and packaged the goods and created a delivery note. The associated delivery note number is the reference that the vendor uses in the shipping notification. You can also select the confirmation category via the selection field (see Figure 2.28).

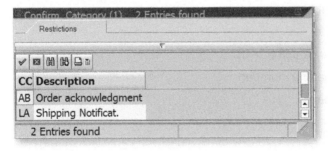

Figure 2.28: Entering a shipping notification: confirmation category

Figure 2.29 shows further relevant data that you have to enter now:

▶ Confirmation category (CC)

▶ Delivery date

▶ Reference

▶ Creation date

You can then save the purchase order as usual.

Delivery	Invoice	Conditions	Account Assignment	Texts	Delivery Address	C

Conf. Control			Confirmations		Order Ack.	
CC	D	Delivery Date	Time	Quantity	Reference	Created on
LA	T	16.10.2016		20	123456	02.09.2016
LA	T	26.10.2016		30	32569	05.09.2016

Figure 2.29: Entering a shipping notification: delivery data

Process Security through order acknowledgments

 In principle, the entry of an order acknowledgment should (also) be mandatory. If there are any deviations between the customer and vendor data, this allows early clarification and entry of the correct data in the SAP system, thus avoiding subsequent correction during invoice verification, for example. If clarification takes place at a later stage, this often leads to late payments, which has a negative impact on business relationships with vendors and in severe cases, delivery blocks.

2.5.2 Posting the goods receipt

Via the path SAP MENU • LOGISTICS • MATERIALS MANAGEMENT • INVENTORY MANAGEMENT • GOODS MOVEMENT • GOODS RECEIPT • FOR PURCHASE ORDER • MIGO—PO NUMBER KNOWN, you can access the screen where you can post the goods receipt.

Alternatively, you can enter transaction MIGO directly to display the view shown in Figure 2.30:

Goods Receipt		Purchase Order					Plant	

General Vendor %

Document Date	05.09.2016	Delivery Note	
Posting Date	05.09.2016	Bill of Lading	
☐ Individual Slip		GR/GI Slip No.	

Figure 2.30: Posting the goods receipt: initial view

When you enter the purchase order number, the system fills further relevant fields by default as soon as you click EXECUTE ⊕. The default posting date is the current date.

In this area, the entry of the delivery note number is particularly important, above all, if further processes, e. g., the credit memo procedure, are to be referenced to it (see Figure 2.31).

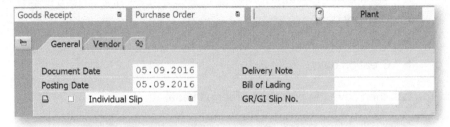

Figure 2.31: Posting the goods receipt: delivery note number

In addition to the delivery note number ❶, in this view you can also define further information about the bill of lading ❷, or, for example, vendor's notes on the delivery note, in the header text ❸. The default document and posting date ❹ is the current date.

Process security through careful data entry

 The importance of entering the delivery note number correctly must be stressed to the warehouse employees. For clarification with the vendor in particular, it is important to be able to use this reference for system searches.

It is not only an accurate entry that is important, but also the observance of formal conventions.

Further entries are now necessary to enable the goods receipt posting. These include, as shown in Figure 2.32, the storage location.

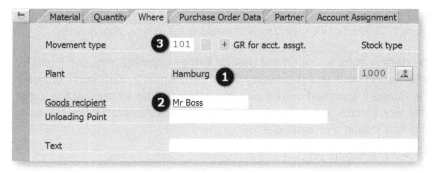

Figure 2.32: Posting the good receipt: entering the storage location

The STORAGE LOCATION ❶ specifies where the goods are to be stored. This can be an area in a general warehouse or, for example, a different company location. In this example, the GOODS RECIPIENT ❷ entry is defaulted through direct entry in the purchase requisition/purchase order. This ensures that the correct contact person receives the goods. This activity also shows that entering the data carefully and completely at the beginning of the process simplifies the subsequent process steps and reduces any time lost with queries, for example.

If you select transaction MIGO PO—NUMBER KNOWN, the MOVEMENT TYPE ❸ is also filled by default. The movement type controls the subsequent processes. For example, the goods receipt can be canceled using movement type 102.

Figure 2.33 shows the entry of the delivery note quantity and the actual quantity delivered thus posted as a goods receipt.

Figure 2.33: Posting the goods receipt: entering the delivery note quantity

The default entry in the QTY IN UNIT OF ENTRY (quantity in quantity unit for order entry) field is the quantity from the shipping notification entered. The quantity specified on the delivery note must be entered at the same time. For various reasons, this can deviate from the quantity on the shipping notification. For example:

► Packaging units

► Loss of or damage to packages

► Input errors

In order to enable differences to be identified more quickly, the number of containers should also be entered.

You can now post the goods receipt by clicking 💾 .

2.5.3   View the purchase order history

If you follow the path SAP MENU • LOGISTICS • MATERIALS MANAGEMENT • PURCHASING • PURCHASE ORDER • DISPLAY, as already described, the view of the last purchase order that you called up appears (see Figure 2.34).

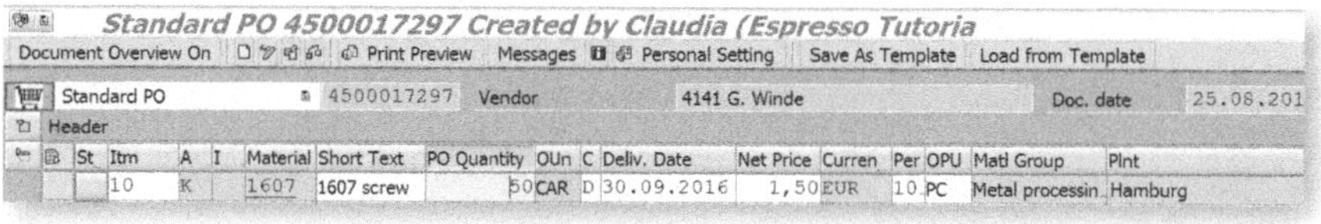

Figure 2.34: Posting the goods receipt, displaying the purchase order

In the item details (see Figure 2.35), select the PURCHASE ORDER HISTO-RY tab:

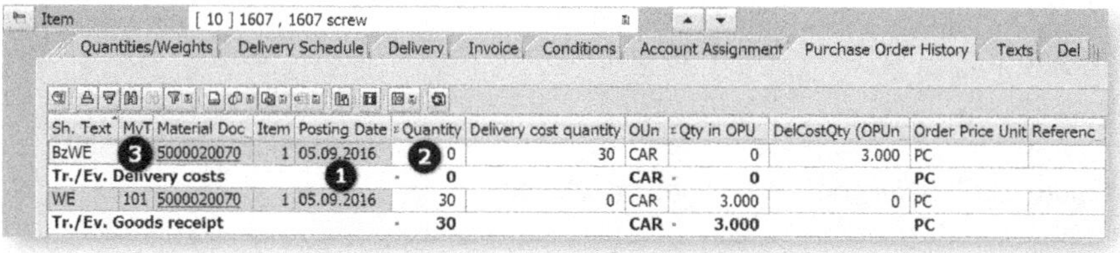

Figure 2.35: Posting the goods receipt: purchase order history

In the purchase order history, after the goods receipt has been posted, you can see that the material has arrived and has been accepted. In addition to the posting date ❶, the quantity ❷ is displayed, together with the movement type ❸ with which the goods were transferred to the company stock. For a goods receipt for a standard purchase order, the movement type is 101: the notification of goods receipt.

In some cases, it is useful for the person ordering the materials to receive a notification as soon as the goods receipt is posted. Reasons for this include:

▶ Delivery of particularly valuable materials

▶ Delivery of materials essential for continued production

▶ Delivery by new or unreliable vendors

▶ Checking new processes—for example, evaluated receipt settlement

In this case, in the purchase order header, you can select the GR MES-SAGE checkbox (see Figure 2.36). This is particularly useful if you want to check the goods receipts during daily business.

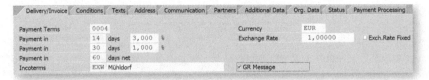

Figure 2.36: Notification of goods receipt: selecting the goods receipt message checkbox

As soon as a goods receipt is posted, you can access a corresponding document in the BUSINESS WORKPLACE.

Figure 2.37: Selecting the business workplace

In the EASY ACCESS menu, click ⟳ (see Figure 2.37) to open the BUSINESS WORKPLACE (see Figure 2.38).

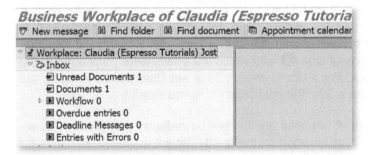

Figure 2.38: Business workplace inbox

In Windows Explorer, you can select the desired document and double-click it to open it (see Figure 2.39).

Figure 2.39: Message in the business workplace

The file contains all of the important information about this goods receipt and you can now check the current stock situation (see Figure 2.40).

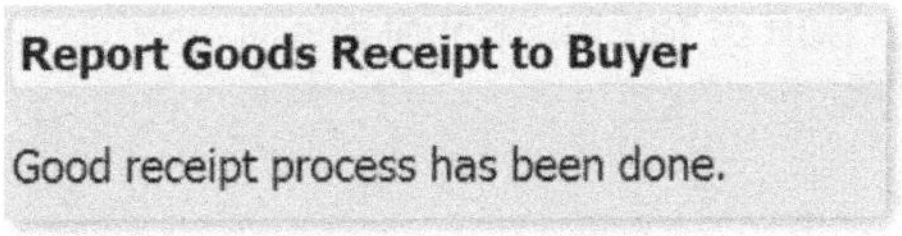

Report Goods Receipt to Buyer

Good receipt process has been done.

Figure 2.40: Notification of goods receipt

In the SAP system, for each *job* set you can send this notification of goods receipt to the vendor via fax or e-mail from the system. This means that your business partner receives prompt information that the goods delivered have arrived and have been posted in your system.

If you are expecting multiple goods receipts for one purchase order but only want to monitor the first delivery, you can deselect the GR MESSAGE checkbox (see Figure 2.36).

2.6 Incoming invoice verification

From an organizational perspective, the incoming invoice verification is also not part of materials management and is often assigned to accounting. The ordering unit must be separate from the settling unit. Again, this is to ensure observance of the principle of segregation of duties. Nevertheless, I will still present the incoming invoice verification check to show you what effects creating a purchase order have on this subsequent process.

2.6.1 Posting the invoice

Incoming invoice verification differentiates between formal and functional accuracy of the invoice. Formal accuracy includes:

▶ Address of the service recipient and service provider

▶ Tax number of the service provider and, if applicable, the sales tax identification number

▶ Date of issue

▶ Invoice number

▶ Quantity, type, and time of service provision/delivery

▶ Tax rate to be applied and the corresponding tax amounts

The following points are checked as part of the functional check:

- ▶ Purchase order number
- ▶ Price and price unit
- ▶ Quantity
- ▶ Total amount
- ▶ Terms of payment
- ▶ Incoterms

If the goods receipt-based invoice verification is activated, the invoice can only be posted if the provision of the service is confirmed by the goods receipt posting.

You can access the incoming invoice verification transaction via the following path: LOGISTICS • MATERIALS MANAGEMENT• LOGISTICS INVOICE VERIFICATION • DOCUMENT ENTRY • ENTER INVOICE. Alternatively, you can call up transaction MIRO directly.

Here, you can enter the purchase order number as a preselection again (see Figure 2.41) and import the data from the purchase order by pressing **Enter**.

PO Reference	G/L Account	Material						

Purchase Order/Scheduling Agreement	▤	4500017297		⇨	🗑		Goods/service items
						Layout	All Information

Item	Amount	Quantity		Ord	⇩	Purchase order	Item	PO Text
1	45,00			30 CAR	☐	4500017297	10	1607 screw
2	15,00			20 CAR	☐	4500017297	10	1607 screw

Figure 2.41: Incoming invoice verification: entering the purchase order number

The following view (see Figure 2.42) shows that a large number of the relevant fields are already filled in for this function as well.

❶ In the BASIC DATA area you enter the INVOICE DATE. This can deviate from the current date—for example, to clear invoices that have been posted late and taking account of the payment target.

❷ You can also enter a different POSTING DATE. However, this is more relevant for financial accounting in order to post all relevant transactions in the correct period as part of closing activities.

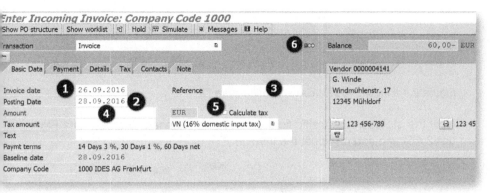

Figure 2.42: Incoming invoice verification: basic data

❸ The REFERENCE is the vendor's invoice number. This should also be transferred so that any subsequent clarification necessary with the vendor can be conducted with little effort.

❹ The AMOUNT corresponds to the invoice amount that the vendor specifies on the invoice.

❺ The TAX AMOUNT can be determined via the input VAT (sales tax) indicator. In this case, you have to activate the CALCULATE TAX checkbox and select an input VAT (sales tax) indicator, although the tax amount can also be transferred from the vendor invoice.

❻ The traffic light display in the BALANCE area indicates that information is still missing and you still cannot post the invoice yet; you have to enter further information for the item (see Figure 2.43).

Figure 2.43: Incoming invoice verification: G/L account

In addition to the information about the G/L account, you can also define or check further information for the material. Figure 2.44 shows the subsequent indication of the item with status OK 🔄.

Figure 2.44: Incoming invoice verification: item OK

Now the status in the traffic light display has changed to green (see Figure 2.45) and you can post the invoice.

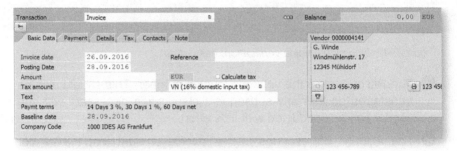

Figure 2.45: Incoming invoice verification: posting the invoice

The incoming invoice verification also clearly shows how important it is to provide correct system data with all relevant information.

2.6.2 View the purchase order history

You can also look at changes in the purchase order history in the purchase order view. You call up the purchase order view with transaction ME23N.

The situation as shown in Figure 2.46 arises after the incoming invoice has been posted. In addition to the POSTING DATE ❶, the QUANTITY ❷ is displayed, as well as the ORDERING UNIT ❸ with which the goods are invoiced by the vendor. You can use the INVOICE DOCUMENT NUMBER ❹ to call up further information for this posting transaction.

To complete this order transaction and identify the purchase order for archiving, you can now activate the DELIVERY COMPLETE (see Figure 2.47) and FINAL INVOICE (see Figure 2.48) checkboxes.

Sh. Text	MvT	Material Doc	Item	Posting Date	Σ Quantity	Delivery cost quantity	OUn	Σ Qty in OPU	DelCostQty (OPUn	Order Price Unit	Referenc
BzWE		5000020080	1	28.09.2016	0		20	CAR	0	1.000	PC	
BzWE		5000020070	1	05.09.2016	0		30	CAR	0	3.000	PC	
Tr./Ev. Delivery costs					0			CAR	0		PC	
WE	101	5000020080	1	28.09.2016	20		0	CAR	1.000	0	PC	
WE	101	5000020070	1	05.09.2016	30		0	CAR	3.000	0	PC	
Tr./Ev. Goods receipt					50			CAR	4.000		PC	
RE-L		5105608884	1	28.09.2016	30		0	CAR	3.000	0	PC	
RE-L		5105608884	2	28.09.2016	20		0	CAR	1.000	0	PC	
Tr./Ev. Invoice receipt					50			CAR	4.000		PC	

Figure 2.46: Incoming invoice verification: purchase order history

Figure 2.47: Incoming invoice verification, DELIV. COMPL. indicator

Figure 2.48: Incoming invoice verification, FINAL INVOICE indicator

On one hand, this maintenance of completed purchase orders helps to keep the database clean. On the other hand, it also enables the identification of purchase orders that no longer belong to the category, open purchase orders. This supports the reporting of correct key performance indicators.

3 Process optimizations

The standard SAP system already offers tools and predefined processes to make your daily work easier or to ensure greater security
and consistency in process flows. The following chapter contains
selected examples of such processes.

3.1 The release process

This process in an SAP system is designed to ensure that purchase
requisitions or purchase orders are released correctly. The organization
within the company usually defines which purchase orders or purchase
requisitions have to be released by which persons or functions. This is
an authority which allows the employee to execute regularly recurring
legal transactions. The range of the authority is generally defined in the
contract of employment or job description.

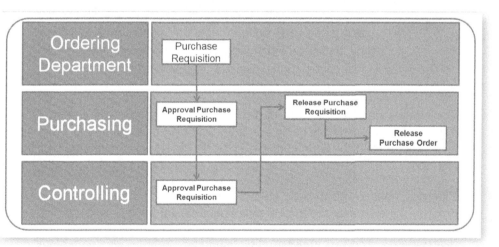

Figure 3.1: Flow of the release process

Another form of authority is the *power of procuration*, which grants the
employee an extensive power of representation. However, these authori-
ties do not generally nullify the principle of dual control (also referred to
as segregation of duties). The authorized signatories act on behalf of the

company and by granting a release, document the legality of a transaction (see Figure 3.1). The release can be granted by means of a signature on the purchase order or via a process in the SAP system.

A system-based release prevents a procurement transaction from being completed prematurely, for example, the printing or sending of a purchase order via electronic data interchange (EDI). This only takes place when the system initiates the execution of the corresponding transaction.

In addition to aspects of this process which are relevant for audit purposes, such as the principle of dual control and compliance with value limits, note also that a paper-based release of purchase orders (signature of the person responsible on the purchase order) involves a significant amount of effort which often takes up a lot of time. And in addition, a piece of paper can get lost.

Release level

 A release strategy can be created not only for purchase requisitions but also for purchase orders, contracts, and outline agreements. The level at which the release takes place in the SAP system depends on the company strategy. However, in principle, the recommendation is to select a level which does not necessitate any further releases.

The release can be activated by both the line manager, who confirms that the correct goods are being procured, and by the person responsible for the cost center, who confirms that the costs are authorized or planned.

Different release strategies should be used for different material groups—for example, production material or capital goods—and also for organizational units. The strategies are based on the different purchasing document types. Some standard document types are already predefined in the SAP system. By way of example, I will explain the *standard purchase order*, the *stock transport order*, and the *frame order*.

▶ You can use the *standard purchase order* for all materials and services.

▶ The *stock transport order* is used for the delivery of goods and services from one (SAP) plant to another.

▶ The *frame order* is used to group multiple procurement transactions and thus reduce the effort involved in individual processing.

▶ In *customizing*, you can add further document types required by the respective organization at any point in time. The document types are usually differentiated by the number range.

▶ The *release strategy* also specifies the order in which release should take place—for example, specific department release before financial release. You can also create different items with different release strategies within one purchase requisition. How useful this is or whether it actually makes the process more difficult depends on the organization.

In the next section, we will look at the activities that you have to perform in customizing.

Structuring the release strategy

 Before you begin configuring the settings in SAP Customizing, you should map the organizational environment and define the roles in the release process. This helps you to avoid any conflicts and inconsistencies at a later point in time.

3.1.1 Customizing for the release process

To continue the example, we will use the following organizational structure (see Figure 3.2).

When implementing the release process in an SAP system, you have to define a *release strategy* first. The procedure for creating this strategy is described below, without any classification (see Figure 3.3).

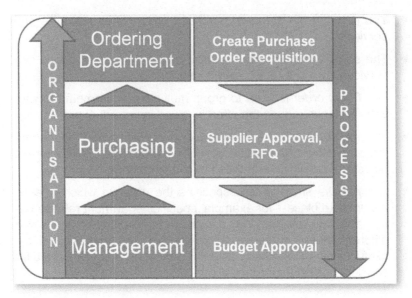

Figure 3.2: Release structure

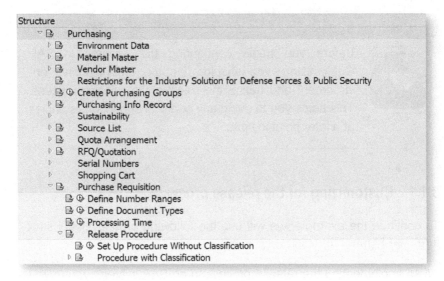

Figure 3.3: Release procedure: initial customizing screen

When you select the item SET UP PROCEDURE WITHOUT CLASSIFICATION, the screen shown below opens (see Figure 3.4).

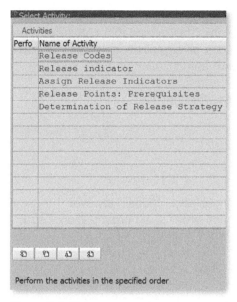

Figure 3.4: Release procedure: process steps

Here you can see the individual steps that you have to process in the order specified:

1. Define the release codes (see Figure 3.5)

2. Create the release indicator (see Figure 3.6)

3. Assign the release indicator (see Figure 3.7)

4. Define the release point prerequisites (see Figure 3.8)

5. Determine the release strategy (see Figure 3.9)

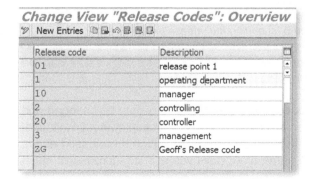

Figure 3.5: Release procedure: defining the release codes

The *release code* is the identification code used to release the purchase requisition or purchase requisition item. This means that certain release codes are assigned to certain persons or organizational units. This assignment is defined as part of the SAP authorization profile.

For example, the release code can be assigned to:

1   The operating department

2   Controlling

3   Management

In theory, you can define up to eight release codes. However, I think it would be difficult to create a purchase order in an organizational structure that is nested to that level.

Save the setting by clicking the SAVE icon.

You can now go back by clicking ⬅. This takes you to the overview of the steps to be completed. Now select the next item, RELEASE INDICATOR (see Figure 3.6).

Change View "Release Indicator": Overview

New Entries

Release ID	Description
1	Request for quotation
2	RFQ/purchase order
3	RFQ/PO no change of date
4	RFQ/PO no changes
A	Fixed RFQ
B	Fixed RFQ/purchase order
S	Blocked

Figure 3.6: Release procedure: changing the release indicator

Release indicators indicate whether the purchase requisition can be changed once it has been released.

The company defines, for example, whether prices may be changed and if so, to what extent. For instance, a price reduction without limitation, that is, without requiring that the purchase requisition be released again, could be allowed. At the same time, however, a price increase of maximum +10% is accepted. If the price is increased by more than 10%, the release has to be processed again.

Figure 3.7 shows an overview of the release indicators for release strategy **R1**, for example.

Change View "Assign Release Indicators": Overview

New Entries

Rel.Str.	C1	C2	C3	C4	C5	C6	C7	C8	Rel. ID	Description
J1	X								1	Request for quotation
J1	X	X							4	RFQ/PO no changes
J1	X	X	X						B	Fixed RFQ/purchase order
R1	X								1	Request for quotation
R1	X	X							2	RFQ/purchase order
S1	X								2	RFQ/purchase order
ZG									S	Blocked

Figure 3.7: Release procedure: assigning the release indicator

▶ Release indicator **1**: The function/person to which release code C1 is assigned has released the request for quotation. In our example, this is the manager of the person making the requisition. Release indicator B: The purchase requisition or RFQ has now been released by the function/person to which release code C2 was assigned. In our example, controlling has granted the financial release. No further date changes are permitted in the purchase order.

In the next step, you have to define the order of the releases (see Figure 3.8).

Change View "Release Points: Prerequisites": Overview

Simulate release   New Entries   Copy as...   Delete   Print standard list   Select All   Select block   Deselect All

Rel.Strat.	Release code	Description	C1	C2	C3	C4	C5	C6	C7	C8
J1	1	operating department	X							
J1	2	controlling	+	X						
J1	3	management	+	+	X					
R1	10	manager	X							
R1	20	controller	+	X						
S1	01	release point 1	X							

Figure 3.8: Release procedure: release point prerequisites

By defining the release sequence, you can map organizational conditions. It also allows you to prevent, for example, the financial release being granted before the department has decided that the purchase requisition has been created for the correct goods.

If the sequence were not defined, the table of the release indicators would be correspondingly long and thus difficult to manage.

In the next step, you have to define the criteria that form the basis for the release strategy being applied for a purchase order (see Figure 3.9).

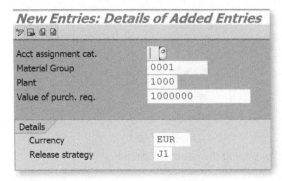

Figure 3.9: Release procedure: defining parameters to be applied

You can define the following parameters:

- ▶ ACCOUNT ASSIGNMENT CATEGORY: The account assignment category determines the cost objects to which the purchase order is posted. These cost objects can be cost centers, projects, or customer orders, for example. As part of the release strategy, you can define, for instance, that purchase orders posted to a customer order have to be released by the sales department. In the same way, you could also create a separate release strategy for each project to ensure that releases are granted by the project manager.

- ▶ MATERIAL GROUP: The material group represents a classification of all materials used in the company. The material groups can be used to define procurement strategies or, for example, to create conditions at a higher level. (See also Section 4.1). The use of the material group to define the release strategy can also be used to assign purchase orders to certain departments. For example, all purchase orders for computers could be assigned to the IT department.

- ▶ PLANT: The assignment to a plant means that the release strategy valid for this organizational unit in the company is applied. The decisive factor would be that this release strategy controls the higher level release by management—for example, the plant manager.

▶ VALUE OF PURCH. REQ.: On one hand, determining the release strategy based on the value of the purchase requisition ensures that purchase orders above a defined amount are triggered exclusively by authorized persons. On the other hand, for significant amounts, this basis ensures the principle of dual control. Conversely, it also indicates that purchase orders below a defined value limit are not subject to a release strategy.

▶ CURRENCY: You have to define a currency because amounts without a currency do not represent a definitive statement about the value of the purchase order or purchase requisition. It is also feasible to imagine that for valuable materials—for example, raw materials such as ores or oil—which are procured in a foreign currency at daily prices, the release ensures the correct currency exchange rate is used.

▶ RELEASE STRATEGY: Here you enter the code for the release strategy.

In the last step (see Figure 3.10), the green checkmark in the process overview shows that you have performed all steps for creating the release strategy correctly.

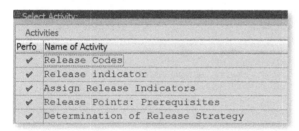

Figure 3.10: Release procedure creation process completed

I am sure that you will now be asking whether you have understood this correctly, and here, is it actually only the results of your previous activity that are displayed? Exactly! This overview confirms that you have thought of everything. That is not always the case in other processes in an SAP system and in the event of an error, extensive research may be necessary.

3.2 Automatic conversion of purchase requisitions into purchase orders

In the context of the process for the purchase order release, the automatic conversion of purchase requisitions into purchase orders represents a further opportunity for optimization. You can do this for all purchase requisitions to which a unique source of supply has already been assigned. If there are multiple potential sources of supply for goods to be procured, the SAP system can determine the valid vendor via source list entries, regular vendors, or quota arrangements, for example.

To execute the purchase requisition conversion process, the automatic creation of purchase orders must be released for this vendor in the vendor master (see Figure 3.11). To do this, call up transaction MK02 or choose the following path in customizing: LOGISTICS • MATERIALS MANAGEMENT • PURCHASING • MASTER DATA • VENDOR • PURCHASING • CHANGE (CURRENT).

You can find this setting on the PURCHASING DATA tab, under CONTROL DATA.

Control data

☑ GR-Based Inv. Verif.	ABC indicator	
☑ AutoEvalGRSetmt Del.	ModeOfTrnsprt-Border	
☐ AutoEvalGRSetmt Ret	Office of entry	
☑ Acknowledgment Reqd	Sort criterion	By VSR sequence number
☑ Automatic purchase order	PROACT control prof.	
☐ Subsequent settlement	☐ Revaluation allowed	
☐ Subseq. sett. index	☐ Grant discount in kind	
☐ B.vol.comp./ag.nec.	☐ Relevant for Price Det. (Vendor Hierarchy)	
☐ Doc. index active	☐ Relevant for agency business	
☐ Returns vendor		
☐ Srv.-Based Inv. Ver.	Shipping Conditions	

Figure 3.11: Automatic conversion of purchase requisitions: vendor master

You also have to set the AUTOMATIC PURCHASE ORDER indicator for the material.

To do this, call up the material master. Follow the path LOGISTICS • MATERIALS MANAGEMENT • MATERIAL MASTER • MATERIAL – CHANGE or enter transaction MM02.

Once you have called up the transaction, you will see the view shown in Figure 3.12. Now you have to enter the material number that you want to change.

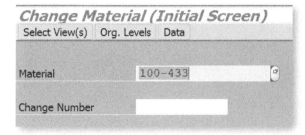

Figure 3.12: Changing the material master record: entering the material number

Once you have confirmed the entry by pressing the ⟨Enter⟩ key or clicking the ✅ icon, you have to enter the organizational data (see Figure 3.13). By linking the material master (which can be valid across multiple organizations) and organizational data—in this case, plant **1000**—you ensure that process changes only come into effect where they have been agreed. Without this link, there would be a risk that process changes introduced in one organization would lead to problems in another organization because changes to basic data which would potentially be required have not been made.

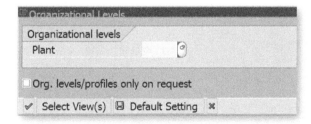

Figure 3.13: Changing the material master: entering the plant

You can then select the views in which the changes are to be made. For our example, this is the PURCHASING view (see Figure 3.14).

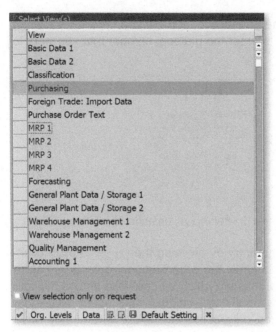

Figure 3.14: Changing the material master: selecting the view

You also have to activate the AUTOM. PO setting in the purchasing view (see Figure 3.15). Once you have saved the view, the material master change is complete.

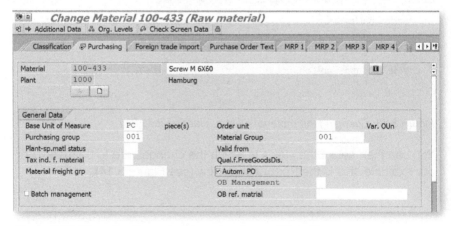

Figure 3.15: Changing the material master: AUTOM PO setting

Basic data for the order transaction

 As is the case for all automated processes, it is also an advantage for the automatic creation of the purchase orders if the basic purchasing data for the goods to be procured and the sources of supply for these goods (including the correct basic data) are provided. This reduces the need for subsequent manual intervention or, in an ideal situation, avoids such intervention completely.

You can call up transaction ME59 directly or access it via the following path: LOGISTICS • MATERIALS MANAGEMENT • PURCHASING • PURCHASE ORDER • CREATE • AUTOMATICALLY VIA PURCHASE REQUISITIONS.

The screen shown in Figure 3.16 appears.

Automatic Creation of Purchase Orders from Requisitions

Purchasing Group	to	⇨
Purchasing Organization	to	⇨
Vendor	to	⇨
Contract	to	⇨
Plant	to	⇨
Supplying Plant	to	⇨

New Purchase Order
- ☐ Per Purchasing Group
- ☐ Per Plant
- ☐ Per Storage Location
- ☐ Per Item Category
- ☑ Per Company Code

- ☐ Per Delivery Date
- ☐ Per Vendor Subrange
- ☐ Per Requisition
- ☐ Per Requisition Item

Other Parameters
- ☐ Generate Schedule Lines
- ☐ Omit Faulty Items
- ☐ Detailed Log

- ☐ Test Run
- 1 Set Requisitions to "Closed"

Figure 3.16: Automatic purchase order conversion: initial screen

In the upper part of the screen, you should define as many selection parameters as possible to obtain a result tailored to your work area. I would like to address the most important of these parameters below:

> ▶ MRP controller or PURCHASING GROUP: only those purchase requisitions that are in your area of responsibility are selected.

▶ PURCHASING ORGANIZATION: defined organizational areas can be excluded from automatic processing.

▶ VENDOR: you can restrict automated processing to vendors for whom, based on experience, the information flow with regard to ordering conditions works without any problem.

▶ PLANT: you can also use this selection to exclude organizational areas within the organization or select them specifically.

In the test system we are using for our example, because of the small amount of data available, simple restrictions are also successful.

You should also define the following parameters in the NEW PURCHASE ORDER area (see Figure 3.17).

New Purchase Order

☐ Per Purchasing Group	☐ Per Delivery Date
☐ Per Plant	☐ Per Vendor Subrange
☐ Per Storage Location	☐ Per Requisition
☐ Per Item Category	☐ Per Requisition Item
☑ Per Company Code	

Figure 3.17: Automatic purchase order: restriction

▶ PER PURCHASING GROUP: purchase orders can be uniquely assigned to a person responsible. (In our example, this selection is not necessary. The purchasing group is in the header data in the purchase order, which means that there will always be one purchase order per purchasing group.)

▶ PER PLANT: with this selection, you ensure that only items for one organizational unit are processed in a purchase order.

▶ PER ITEM CATEGORY (e. g., normal, consignment, subcontracting): if you select this parameter, you reduce the number of potential errors during subsequent processing of the purchase order.

▶ PER DELIVERY DATE: in the case of delivery delays caused by the vendor, this selection ensures that clarifications can be performed for a specific procurement transaction and misunderstandings or queries can be reduced.

▶ PER REQUISITION: assuming that there can be multiple requisitioning parties for one vendor or material, with this setting you guarantee that a purchase order has to be uniquely assigned to a requisitioning party. This is also helpful if clarification is required.

By making a finely structured selection, you can ensure that all correct items are converted into a purchase order without any incorrect items hampering this order transaction. You also define measures that speed up any clarification required.

Creating the purchase order

 For the goods receipt process, it can be an advantage if a separate purchase order is created for each material and, where applicable, for each schedule line. This avoids any confusion when the goods receipt is posted and makes any clarification required easier.

Further settings are also available in the OTHER PARAMETERS area with the following fields (see Figure 3.18):

Figure 3.18: Automatic purchase order: other parameters

▶ OMIT FAULTY ITEMS: if you select this option, the processing of the purchase requisitions does not stop when the system encounters an incorrect item; instead, this item is skipped.

▶ SET REQUISITIONS TO CLOSED: processed purchase requisitions are no longer displayed in the worklist and can be archived.

▶ TEST RUN: at the beginning of the process changeover in particular, it is helpful and sensible to conduct a test run. This gives you a good overview of which purchase requisitions can be converted into a purchase order without any problem and which purchase requisitions cause errors. Analyzing these problems should improve the process and lead to a process flow that does not have any errors.

On the lower part of the screen for creating purchase orders automatically, (see Figure 3.16), which you can access by calling up transaction ME59, you have further interesting selection options (see Figure 3.19):

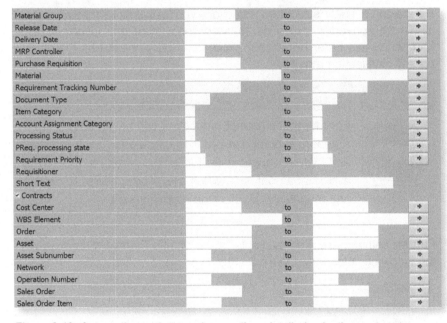

			to		
Material Group			to		➡
Release Date			to		➡
Delivery Date			to		➡
MRP Controller			to		➡
Purchase Requisition			to		➡
Material			to		➡
Requirement Tracking Number			to		➡
Document Type			to		➡
Item Category			to		➡
Account Assignment Category			to		➡
Processing Status			to		➡
PReq. processing state			to		➡
Requirement Priority			to		➡
Requisitioner					
Short Text					
☑ Contracts					
Cost Center			to		➡
WBS Element			to		➡
Order			to		➡
Asset			to		➡
Asset Subnumber			to		➡
Network			to		➡
Operation Number			to		➡
Sales Order			to		➡
Sales Order Item			to		➡

Figure 3.19: Automatic purchase order creation: detailed selection parameters

▶ MATERIAL: in my opinion, you should use this area to exclude materials—for example, materials subject to daily prices. If separate number ranges are assigned in the company for C materials, you can achieve a useful restriction here by selecting only those materials whose material number begins with "C*", for example.

▶ RELEASE DATE: selecting this option can be useful if, for example, you have to comply with value limits at the end of a period.

▶ DELIVERY DATE: the delivery date should be entered if planning reliability is not very high for future requirements.

All of the selection criteria are useful because you can use them to support an automated sequence by means of a regular job.

Limitation

 In addition to selecting the transactions which can be used for the automatic purchase order creation, a limitation can be used to exclude old or unclear transactions. Of course, there should not be any of these in a company but with the number of events arising they are almost unavoidable. Companies with a manageable number of purchase orders will probably not use an SAP system.

As soon as you have entered all of the required parameters, you can start the transaction by clicking ⊕. Figure 3.20 shows the result.

Automatic Creation of Purchase Orders from Requisitions

POrg OTy. Contract		Reqs	PO Item	Message
Vendor 4141				
1000 NB	W/o Contract	1	1	Purchase order 4500017302 Created

Figure 3.20: Automatic purchase order creation: result

With regard to the automated creation of purchase orders, we can say in general that for materials procured on a regular basis, the process is useful in reducing the level of work required. Examples of such materials are C parts, that is, low-value materials, and operating supplies, such as screws, lubricants, or office supplies.

The automatic processing of the purchase order process is also the correct alternative for vendors for whom more complex logistics concepts are too demanding—for example, because the data processing infrastructure is not available or the vendor does not want to have to deal with standardized logistics processes because of a low purchasing volume. It allows the business partner's desire for uncomplicated collaboration to be combined with low-effort processes in their own company.

Another use for the automatic processing is when materials are transferred from one plant to another within a company by means of stock transport orders. The purchase requisition could be created automatically in the receiving plant by setting up a reorder level and then converting the purchase requisitions into purchase orders in a (regular) job. The *reorder level* specifies the stock level plus fixed promised inflows (order acknowledgments and shipping notifications) from which a new procurement has to be triggered. It usually describes the average requirement that has to be covered during the replenishment lead time.

3.3 The credit memo procedure

In an SAP system, there are various credit memo procedures for clearing a delivery or service.

Firstly, there is the credit memo which is based on the **settlement of a goods removal** from the *consignment stock* of the vendor. The prerequisite for this is a consignment agreement with the vendor. Consignment stock means that the goods remain the property of the vendor up until the time of removal but they are stored at the customer's premises. This is a standard process in some industries, such as the automotive industry, but is generally the exception.

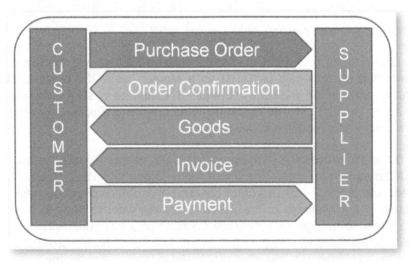

Figure 3.21: Process for a credit memo procedure

When a credit memo is issued for a **delivery of goods or performance of a service**, an agreement also has to be reached with the vendor. However, this is much easier to achieve because it focuses not on the ownership structures but rather on the simplified and automated settlement of delivery and service. Figure 3.21 shows the process of a system-based goods receipt settlement.

The following steps are executed in a credit memo procedure:

1. The customer sends a purchase order as usual. This purchase order must contain the following note: "This purchase order will be settled in a credit memo procedure." This note is important so that the vendor knows that he must not create an invoice for this transaction or must not send an invoice to the customer.

2. The vendor then creates an order acknowledgment which can be used to check the most important order data.

3. In the next step, the vendor sends the goods or performs the service and issues the customer with a delivery note or an activity confirmation.

4. Based on the delivery note number or the activity confirmation number, the customer posts the goods receipt in the SAP system.

5. The settlement of the goods receipts is then triggered and the credit memo is sent to the vendor.

6. The vendor checks whether the credit memo is correct and, if necessary, contacts the customer to request clarification.

3.3.1   Adjusting the vendor master

If purchase orders are to be settled in a credit memo procedure, you have to define the required setting in the vendor master. By doing so, you ensure that all purchase orders for a vendor are already created as an *automatic goods receipt settlement* (also referred to as an *ERS (evaluated receipt settlement) procedure*) by selecting ☑ AutoEvalGRSetmt Del. .

You can select this setting in the vendor master in the purchasing view on the PURCHASING DATA tab in the CONTROL DATA area (see Figure 3.22).

Figure 3.22: ERS setting, vendor master

By activating the ACKNOWLEDGMENT REQD indicator, you ensure that a purchase order confirmation is sent to the vendor. This allows variances to be recognized and eliminated quickly and avoids incorrect settlement.

A further prerequisite for settlement in a credit memo procedure is the activation of the *goods receipt-based invoice verification* by selecting . Goods receipts that are posted for a purchase order without a goods receipt-based invoice verification can no longer be settled in the ERS procedure. In this case, reversing the goods receipt does not help because the GR-BASED INV. VERIF. indicator cannot be selected for a purchase order item retrospectively. If you ever come across this situation, the best thing to do is to reverse the purchase order item, create a new purchase order item, and then settle this item. You have to remove the incorrect item from the settlement table.

Goods receipt-based invoice verification

Purchase orders should always be created with the goods receipt-based invoice verification function. This allows you to ensure that when an invoice is received, the goods have been delivered or the service performed and the invoice can be processed without any further queries.

With regard to auditing (e. g., internal control system [ICS]), having this setting as a default setting is evaluated positively. Colleagues who deliberately do not use this setting often use the greater amount of effort involved as an argument against it. You can counter this argument by stating that no private person would pay an invoice without being sure that the service has been received. Your employer should be able to expect the same secure handling of the company's assets.

3.3.2   Creating the purchase order in the ERS process

When you create the purchase order, all settings configured under Section 3.1.1 are adopted. You may have to enter the tax code **VN** (see Figure 3.23). This ensures that the correct rate of sales tax is used.

The sales tax codes are defined by the company and can be very different in each case. Therefore, the sales tax code used here is merely an example.

Figure 3.23: ERS – tax code in the purchase order

It is important that under CONDITIONS, you do not create any purchase orders with the ESTIMATED PRICE indicator (see Figure 3.24). Settlement would not be possible in this case. Therefore, you have to activate the PRINT PRICE checkbox. This has the effect that the price is printed on the order form that you send to the vendor.

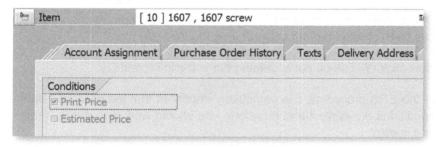

Figure 3.24: Activating the PRINT PRICE ERS indicator

In the service area in particular, it can be useful to send purchase orders without any price specification. For transactions in which it is difficult for the buyer to estimate the actual costs and in case of doubt his estimation will be too high, it can be useful to send a purchase order without specifying a price. This avoids giving the vendor "carte blanche" to calculate the actual price as close to this estimated price as possible even if the actual costs due would be much lower.

Whether this procedure makes sense for every business relationship has to be decided on a case by case basis and depends heavily on the relationship between the business partners. However, it is certainly not possible to get offers from various providers for every transaction in order to achieve a realistic price.

Therefore, if you were to use the ESTIMATED PRICE option, in this case you would have to change the purchase order directly after sending it, that is, deselect the ESTIMATED PRICE option.

At the same time, however, you would have to avoid sending new output. Proceed as follows: in the menu, select the OUTPUT function. Please make sure that you do this before you save the purchase order.

Change Pur. Order :: Output

🔳 🗐 🗓 🔍 Communication method   🞣 Processing log   Further data   Repeat output   Change output

Pur. Order.......... 4500017297

Output

Status	Output T	Description	Medium		Funct	Partner		Lang	Cha	Proc
ᴄᴏᴏ	NEU	ᵉw PO printout	Print output	▣	VN	4141		DE		
				▣						

Figure 3.25: Suppressing ERS output

In the list that appears, select the output that has a yellow triangle in the STATUS column. This yellow triangle indicates that the output concerned has been created but not sent yet (see Figure 3.25).

Now click 🗑. The output is deleted but you can recreate it.

In the ERS procedure it is particularly important that the purchase order conditions are correct and therefore, you should work with the *confirmation control*.

Using the confirmation from the vendor, you can determine whether the correct conditions have been used for the purchase order. If there are any variances, these can be clarified quickly before the goods are received.

As long as no order acknowledgment has been created, you can use the confirmation control in defined frequencies to create an order acknowledgment reminder for the vendor. Once an order acknowledgment has been entered, there is no further reminder.

Order acknowledgment reminder

 Because a reminder is created if no order acknowledgment has been entered in the SAP system, it makes sense to select a frequency that allows you sufficient time to process any order acknowledgments received. Otherwise you may end up sending reminders for order acknowledgments that have already been in your in-tray for a few days. This risk should not be underestimated, particularly in situations where employees are standing in for other employees who are on vacation, for example.

The optimal solution is automated processing of order acknowledgments: this can be done using an EDI system or via scanning and IT-based processing.

3.3.3 The purchasing info record in the ERS process

In principle, it makes sense to create a *purchasing info record* in all cases in which material or a service is purchased multiple times. In the purchasing info record, you assign a material to a vendor and you can define procurement-related data valid specifically for this vendor. When you create a purchase order for the material from this vendor, this data is then used per default. This data can include:

► Price and price validity

► Delivery time

► Vendor's material number

► Etc.

For more detailed information about the purchasing info record, see Section 4.2.

In the context of the credit memo procedure, you can use the purchasing info record to default to the correct purchase order parameters (see Figure 3.26).

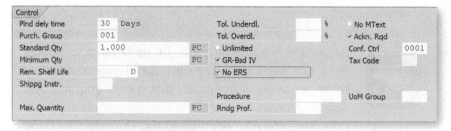

Control						
Plnd dely time	30 Days		Tol. Underdl.		%	☐ No MText
Purch. Group	001		Tol. Overdl.		%	☑ Ackn. Rqd
Standard Qty	1.000	PC	☐ Unlimited			Conf. Ctrl	0001
Minimum Qty		PC	☑ GR-Bsd IV			Tax Code
Rem. Shelf Life	D		☑ No ERS			
Shippg Instr.						
			Procedure			UoM Group
Max. Quantity		PC	Rndg Prof.			

Figure 3.26: ERS info record settings

In addition to the ACKN. REQD and CONF. CTRL indicators, you must also activate the GR-BSD IV indicator.

A special feature here is the option to exclude materials in the purchasing info record from the credit memo procedure.

Excluding materials from the credit memo procedure

Before using this option, you should always check whether there is any other option for processing the purchase order and settlement for these materials. Every deviation from the standard leads to queries and processes that are not handled correctly and therefore delays.

3.3.4   Settling goods receipts

You start the settlement of a goods receipt via the following path: LOGISTICS • MATERIALS MANAGEMENT • LOGISTICS INVOICE VERIFICATION • AUTOMATIC SETTLEMENT • EVALUATED RECEIPT SETTLEMENT. Alternatively, call up the settlement directly using transaction MRRL.

The view shown in Figure 3.27 appears.

Here you should enter information in at least the following fields:

- ▶ COMPANY CODE
- ▶ GOODS RECEIPT POSTING DATE

With these settings you can settle, for example, the goods receipts of the previous week. Because only those goods receipts for which the ERS indicator is selected are included in the worklist, you do not have to make any further selections here.

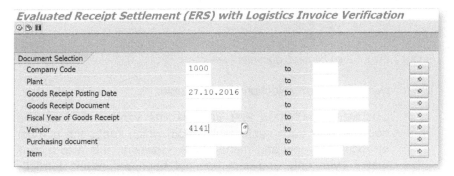

Document Selection			
Company Code	1000	to	
Plant		to	
Goods Receipt Posting Date	27.10.2016	to	
Goods Receipt Document		to	
Fiscal Year of Goods Receipt		to	
Vendor	4141	to	
Purchasing document		to	
Item		to	

Figure 3.27: ERS settlement: selection variables

As already described in Section 3.2 on creating purchase orders automatically, further selections may still be helpful in order to exclude old or irrelevant transactions. For organizational reasons, it makes sense to enter the vendor numbers because accounting employees are often assigned to specific vendors.

It also makes sense to create a *variant* here (see Section 4.3). If the date was created dynamically, the settlement can take place via an SAP job; the employee does not have to trigger it.

Of course, settlements for a purchase order or a vendor can take place outside the agreed frequency or at the end of the fiscal year.

In this case, the document selections are important (see Figure 3.28). These have significant effects on the number of documents selected and settlements will potentially not be performed. The greater the number of goods receipt postings settled within a document, the lower the number of settlement documents—for example, only one per vendor and settlement period. Initially, this sounds very appealing. However, this selection also bears the great risk that the settlement cannot be performed because there is an error in a goods receipt posting—for example, the ESTIMATED PRICE checkbox is activated in the purchase order. This would prevent the entire settlement for possibly hundreds of goods receipts.

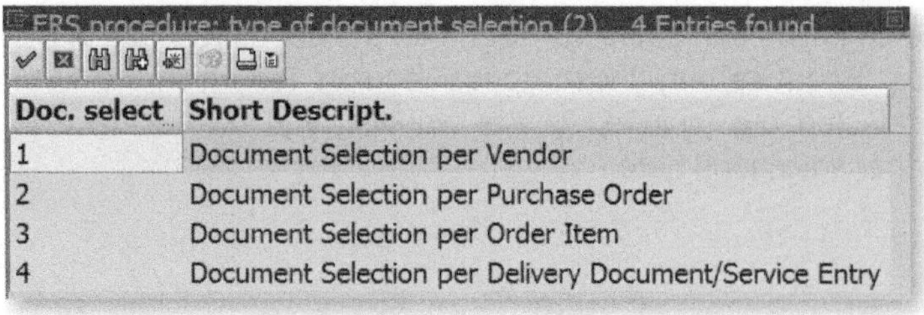
ERS procedure: type of document selection (2)   4 Entries found

Doc. select	Short Descript.
1	Document Selection per Vendor
2	Document Selection per Purchase Order
3	Document Selection per Order Item
4	Document Selection per Delivery Document/Service Entry

Figure 3.28: ERS settlement: document selection

The following document selections are available:

- DOCUMENT SELECTION PER VENDOR: the vendor receives one document for each settlement period, which keeps the number of documents low and manageable. However, this also means that if even only one item has not been processed correctly (e.g., missing input tax code), the entire settlement cannot be performed. In the case of vendors with large volumes in particular, this can lead to discussions and in the worst case, to a delivery stop.
- DOCUMENT SELECTION PER PURCHASE ORDER: for each settlement period, the vendor receives one settlement for the purchase orders for which a goods receipt was posted within the settlement period. The number of documents is greater than in the first case but still relatively manageable.
- DOCUMENT SELECTION PER ORDER ITEM: with this selection, the vendor receives a settlement for each purchase order item to which a goods receipt has been posted. There are more settlements than in the previous case. In a project business with a strongly varying number of purchase order items, this selection can be practical because it is not based on a regular production supply.
- DOCUMENT SELECTION PER DELIVERY DOCUMENT/SERVICE ENTRY: this setting takes account of vendors who may group deliveries and deliver them with one collective delivery note. With this type of settlement, the vendor can compare the settlement with his own delivery note and any potential corresponding invoice created internally.

It is worth testing during the pilot phase which document selection is most useful. This depends, on one hand, on the number of transactions and the resulting accumulation of documents, but on the other hand, also on how disciplined the internal colleagues are with regard to the process. If settlements have to be clarified frequently because, for example, prices have not been updated or goods receipts not posted, one settlement per purchase order or per purchase order item is recommended.

You can now start the settlement in a *test run* `Test Run` (this icon appears on the SAP screen once you have called up transaction MRRL). The result is a list which shows which goods receipts were posted without errors and what errors there are in the goods receipts that cannot be settled (see Figure 3.29).

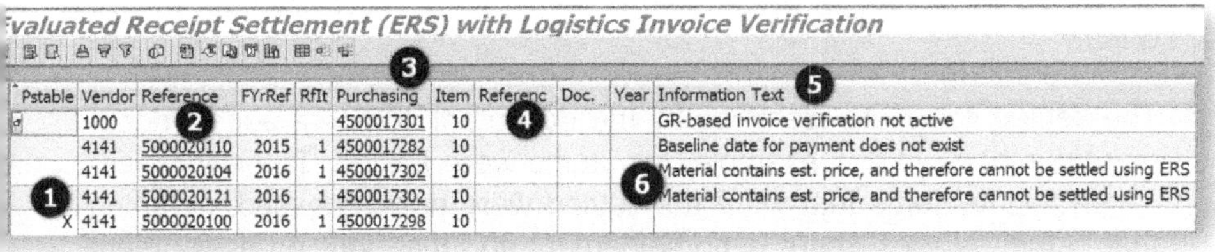

Pstable	Vendor	Reference	FYrRef	RfIt	Purchasing	Item	Referenc	Doc.	Year	Information Text
	1000				4500017301	10				GR-based invoice verification not active
	4141	5000020110	2015	1	4500017282	10				Baseline date for payment does not exist
	4141	5000020104	2016	1	4500017302	10				Material contains est. price, and therefore cannot be settled using ERS
	4141	5000020121	2016	1	4500017302	10				Material contains est. price, and therefore cannot be settled using ERS
X	4141	5000020100	2016	1	4500017298	10				

Valuated Receipt Settlement (ERS) with Logistics Invoice Verification

Figure 3.29: ERS result: test run

❶ The items which can be settled without errors are marked with **X**.

❷ The document shown in the REFERENCE (DOCUMENT) column is the goods receipt document. Click the document number to switch directly to the document display.

❸ The PURCHASING (DOCUMENT) column contains the purchase order number and the item to be settled. Here too you can click the purchase order number to switch directly to the purchase order display. You cannot use the DISPLAY/CHANGE PURCHASE ORDER 🖉 icon in this case. When you start the goods receipt settlement the purchase order enters the **In Progress** status. Before you can make changes to purchase orders, you have to close the goods receipt settlement for this purchase order.

❹ If settlement has been performed successfully, this column contains the number of the FI document.

❺ INFORMATION TEXT: in this field, the SAP system shows information about why a settlement could not be performed. In this example, the GOODS RECEIPT-BASED INVOICE VERIFICATION checkbox was not activated in the purchase order. Therefore, no ERS settlement can take place.

❻ Here we see another example of an error message. It states that for this line item, the ESTIMATED PRICE checkbox is activated. Before the ERS procedure can be completed, you have to deactivate this checkbox.

The information from the error messages displayed can now be passed on to the specific departments for errors to be eliminated, where applicable, or in the case of errors that cannot be eliminated, for consultation with the vendor on how to proceed.

When you deselect the test run option, the list of settled items and purchase orders, including the invoice documents, is displayed (see Figure 3.30).

The settled items are identified by the document numbers and FI document numbers. In this example, two items were settled. The error messages for the items that were not settled were not processed, meaning that in these cases, there is no settlement and therefore no assignment of FI document numbers.

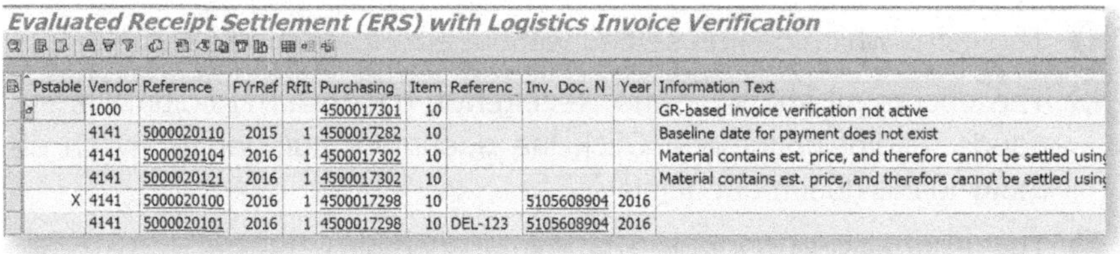

	Pstable	Vendor	Reference	FYrRef	Rflt	Purchasing	Item	Referenc	Inv. Doc. N	Year	Information Text
		1000				4500017301	10				GR-based invoice verification not active
		4141	5000020110	2015	1	4500017282	10				Baseline date for payment does not exist
		4141	5000020104	2016	1	4500017302	10				Material contains est. price, and therefore cannot be settled usin
		4141	5000020121	2016	1	4500017302	10				Material contains est. price, and therefore cannot be settled usin
	X	4141	5000020100	2016	1	4500017298	10		5105608904	2016	
		4141	5000020101	2016	1	4500017298	10	DEL-123	5105608904	2016	

Evaluated Receipt Settlement (ERS) with Logistics Invoice Verification

Figure 3.30: ERS result: settlement

In this list, the reference documents, purchasing documents, and the document number (invoice document) are interactive, meaning that you can open and change these documents from the view.

3.3.5 Vendor agreement about the use of the credit memo procedure

When the credit memo procedure is introduced, a written agreement with the vendor is generally required. On the one hand, this is because the invoicing party is responsible for ensuring the accuracy of the invoice. On the other hand, this agreement between the customer and the vendor defines which document is the leading document for the advance return for tax on sales/purchases.

In the first case, agreement must be reached with the vendor that this changed information will be forwarded to the party issuing the credit memo immediately.

In the second case, when the balances are reconciled at the end of the fiscal year, it must be clear to the auditor from the agreement that the vendor maintains the credit memo document (that is, the reference to the credit memo, the credit memo number) in his own systems, analog to his own invoice numbers. In case of doubt, an Excel table which assigns the credit memo number to the corresponding invoice numbers of the vendor may suffice. However, this must be clarified with the auditor.

At the same time, this agreement must also define who is responsible for creating the correction documents in the case of variances, for example, due to price changes.

The *evaluated receipt settlement* process increases process discipline in the company as a whole and improves collaboration with the vendor. If all parties involved in the process adhere to the specifications, the result is an automated process which drastically reduces the number of documents to be processed in each party's own invoice receipts and limits queries due to "lost" documents to a minimum. At the same time, colleagues are more aware of and disciplined about completing all steps required to process a purchase order. In areas concerned with non-production material in particular, employees often do not take the required care when forwarding documents or posting goods receipts.

From my own experience, I can report that the introduction of the credit memo procedure is triggered less from accounting departments and more from procuring departments. Therefore, if you are thinking about such process improvements in procurement or purchasing, you should consult with two or three vendors who will introduce this process together with you. Of course, you should select vendors with whom you have a good relationship and who have a manageable number of goods receipts.

3.3.6 Tracking changes

For the evaluated receipt settlement process, it is very important that the required basic settings in the master data remain unchanged.

In practice, however, colleagues who are unfamiliar with the credit memo procedure often use the same vendor number and make changes that block this procedure—in particular, they deactivate the GOODS RECEIPT-BASED INVOICE VERIFICATION checkbox referred to in Section 3.3.1. Although activating this checkbox makes sense and, in my opinion, should be a mandatory setting, it is often disabled in order to simplify the invoice process. Many users are obviously not aware that a goods receipt posting is also useful for complete deliveries, services, or non-stock-based materials in order to document the receipt of the goods or the performance of the service. In these cases, important settings in the vendor master or the purchase order may be changed and the process then no longer runs smoothly. This is because these default settings are then no longer used in the subsequent purchase orders and thus decisive parameters are missing for the process.

To find out who has made the changes and why, it can be useful to look at the actions at field level. In the vendor master, you can call up the changes for the ☑ AutoEvalGRSetmt Del. field (see Figure 3.31). To do so, click the field name so that an outline appears around the ☑ AutoEvalGRSetmt Del. field.

In the menu, select ENVIRONMENT and activate the FIELD CHANGES option by double-clicking it. The red outline now disappears. All changes for the field selected are now displayed (see Figure 3.32). If you accidentally deselect the AUTOEVALGRSETMT DEL. indicator when highlighting the text, you have to select it again.

The table contains information about when a change took place and which changes were performed. Double-click the date to open an additional window which shows the ID with which this change was made (see Figure 3.33).

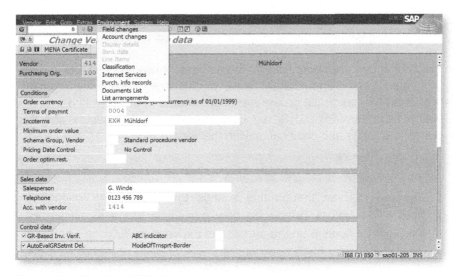

Figure 3.31: Tracking ERS changes: vendor master

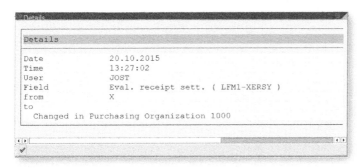

Figure 3.32: ERS: tracking vendor changes: table

Figure 3.33: ERS: tracking vendor changes: ID

You can consult the colleague concerned and find out why these changes were necessary and how they can be avoided in the future.

Such changes are not critical for the settlement process itself as long as they are reversed immediately. However, this step is frequently forgotten. For example, purchase orders are often created in the standard process without the AUTOEVALGRSETMT DEL. indicator being selected and this leads to queries and clarification with the vendor.

Avoiding errors

 Even though this sounds trivial, involving colleagues before introducing new processes has a significant influence on the success of the venture. Anyone who feels they have been passed over or have not received sufficient information will neither support nor help to drive a new process forward. They may even boycott it.

4 Instruments that make work easier, or "From a simple user to a power user"

In the first three chapters, we looked at the basic purchase order process. You can now procure goods or services and know what happens in the goods receipt and settlement areas after a purchase order. You also know the effects of your working methods on these follow-on processes. In the following, you will become familiar with helpful basic data (also referred to as "master data"), functions, and evaluations in the SAP system. These are not essential for daily processing in materials management but they do simplify your working day enormously.

4.1 The material master record—Purchasing and material requirements planning

The SAP material master contains a description of all items that a company procures, produces, and sells. The specific description of an individual material is called the *material master record*. Various departments in the company (e. g., purchasing, material requirements planning, production, accounting, etc.) can access this master record. This prevents redundant data retention and increases overall transparency.

For example, in the material master record, you can see a material's qualification status, that is, whether it is currently being trialed or can be procured without restriction. In the accounting view, you can also see the costs incurred for the material procurement in the last fiscal year via the *MP (moving price)*.

In addition to the multitude of items of data that can be entered for the various specific departments, the data limited to purchasing and material requirements planning is extremely extensive. It also contains various dependencies, the complexity of which cannot be covered in detail in this book. Therefore, you should understand the following explanations on the material master as an encouragement to use the basic data in the SAP system.

In the following I will describe selected master data which is helpful for procurement. You will find this data in the material master records for purchasing and material requirements planning.

The PURCHASING VIEW of the material master record specifies the following:

▶ The purchasing group responsible for the material

▶ The underdelivery and overdelivery limits

▶ The quantity units in which the material may be ordered

The MRP VIEW (MRP = material requirements planning) provides further information for requirements planning. Many of these settings can also be used for pure procurement because, for example, you can specify rounding values which ensure that the correct purchase order quantity (e. g., packaging sizes) is defaulted in the purchase order.

Because material master records are usually created in a central department, I will not describe them here.

You can open and process the material master record via transaction MM02 (see Figure 4.1).

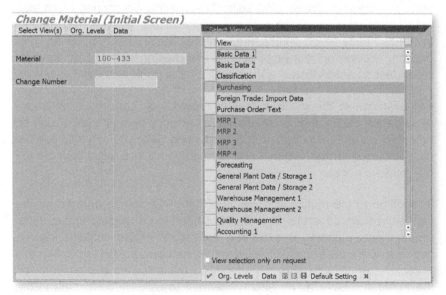

Figure 4.1: Material master: initial screen

Once you have entered the material number, the system prompts you to select the views that you want to display for your working area by clicking the checkboxes. Using the ⊟ Default Setting icon, you can save this selection so that you do not have to enter it again every time you perform any processing or view the material master (transaction MM03).

Once you have confirmed the selection by pressing the Enter key or via ✔ in the menu bar at the very top of the screen, the system prompts you to enter information in the PLANT and STORAGE LOC. fields (see Figure 4.2).

Organizational Levels

Organizational levels

Plant

Storage Loc.

Org. levels/profiles only on request

Select View(s) ⊟ Default Setting ✖

Figure 4.2: Material master: entering the plant and storage location

By entering this information you can create parameters in the material master which are valid for one plant or one storage location exclusively. Whether these restrictions are necessary depends on the organizational structure and the corresponding setup of the SAP system. If, for example, a lot of plants with a different infrastructure access a material master, it may well be useful to specify separate rounding values for these plants in order to take into account the different sizes of storage areas. Just like when selecting the views, by activating the ☐ View selection only on request checkbox, here you can decide (if required) that the selection is to be displayed only on demand.

If you do decide to use this option, note that you may already be displaying other organizational levels or views. In the course of daily business you may have quickly forgotten that you once made this selection. Therefore, if you frequently work in different views or organizational levels, I would recommend that you create a corresponding profile.

If you do not enter a plant or a storage location, when you confirm your entries the data is changed for the entire company and you return to the first view you selected. In our case, that is the PURCHASING VIEW (see Figure 4.3).

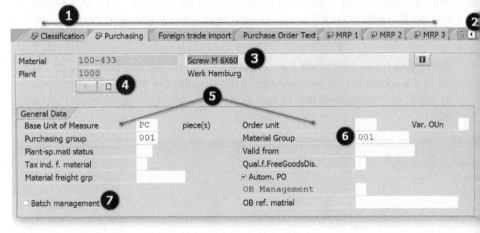

Figure 4.3: Changing the material master: purchasing view

❶ Here you see all the views that exist. If the tab has a green checkmark, this indicates that data has already been created in this view.

❷ You can use the arrows ◄ ► to scroll between the different views. Alternatively, you can use the list selection ☐ to select another view.

❸ The text entered in this field is displayed consistently in the SAP system and on the purchase order. If the field is not locked for entries, I would advise that here you select text that enables other specific departments or substitutes to identify the material easily.

❹ If you work with revision levels, you can access them or display them here.

❺ Here, enter information in the BASE UNIT OF MEASURE and ORDER UNIT fields. This is particularly important for materials which are ordered in packaging units rather than individual units.

Using packaging units

The screws are delivered exclusively in packets of 100 (order unit = CAR). Therefore, if you need 1,000 screws, the system suggests the purchase order quantity "10 CAR". This avoids the vendor accidentally interpreting the purchase order quantity of 1,000 units as 1,000 packages of 100 units.

In this example, the system prompts you to enter the conversion factors (see Figure 4.4).

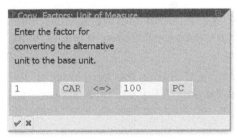

Figure 4.4: Material master: packaging unit conversion factors

❻ By entering a value in the MATERIAL GROUP field, you assign the material to a higher level hierarchy. This makes evaluations easier because, for example, materials for a defined material group can be bundled in one inquiry to the vendor.

❼ Selecting the BATCH MANAGEMENT checkbox indicates that there is a batch management requirement for a material. This is required in particular for perishable goods or for goods subject to technical changes.

The lower part of the purchasing view contains the PURCHASING VALUES and OTHER DATA/MANUFACTURER DATA areas (see Figure 4.5).

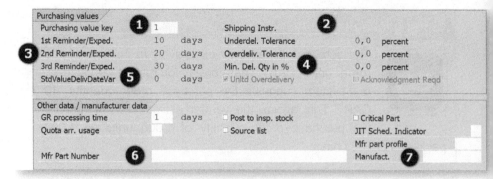

Figure 4.5: Material master: purchasing view, purchasing values

❶ In customizing, the values for the different parameters are assigned to the PURCHASING VALUE KEY. These parameters are specific to the company in which you work. The values displayed here are therefore merely an example.

❷ The entry in the SHIPPING INSTR. field defines the form in which the vendor must package and ship the goods. For example, special hazardous goods packaging may be required, or delivery in a refrigerated truck.

❸ Under (1ST, 2ND, 3RD) REMINDER/EXPED., you define the respective period in which reminders are sent for tender submissions or delivery dates. If a negative figure is entered here, the reminders are sent before the delivery date has expired, for example, and serve merely to jog the recipient's memory.

❹ As part of the vendor rating, this percentage rate indicates the ratio to which a delivery must have taken place to be rated as "successful."

❺ Once the deadline specified here has expired, in the case of a late delivery, the delivery is rated as "not delivered."

❻ and **❼** give you the option of defining a manufacturer part number and the manufacturer.

You can exit this view by selecting another view or by confirming your entries with the ⌈Enter⌋ key.

The following is a limited overview of the helpful entries in the material requirements planning (MRP) views. I will not address the special requirements of system-controlled material requirements planning because these are very complex and to a large extent company-specific.

Material requirements planning view 1

In MATERIAL REQUIREMENTS PLANNING VIEW 1 I would like to highlight the following fields (see Figure 4.6):

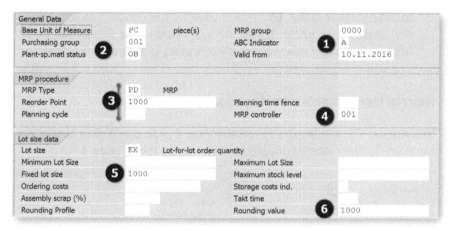

Figure 4.6: Material master: material requirements planning view 1

❶ The ABC INDICATOR corresponds to the common definition used in business management:

A = Important material
B = Material with medium importance
C = Material with low importance

The "importance" can be defined by different factors. The material price is important here, but also whether or not a material can be substituted can be decisive for its classification. For example, a relatively inexpensive material which can only be procured from one vendor can still be an A material.

❷ The entry in the PLANT-SP. MATL. STATUS field indicates whether a material can be procured without limitation or whether, for example, limitations such as a lock apply. The material status is linked to a date. For example, a material lock can apply only from the next calendar year or an unlimited release can be scheduled.

❸ The values defined in the MRP PROCEDURE area are used for system-supported material requirements planning and I will not address them further here. Nevertheless, you should define the codes for the MRP CONTROLLERS ❹ to ensure that the codes are automatically assigned to the correct MRP controllers for evaluations or, for example, when purchase requisitions are created.

❺ The values in the LOT SIZE DATA area are also dependent on the material requirements planning procedure but you can still enter a rounding value under ❻. This is useful if the vendor has fixed delivery units, for example. If you enter a value in the ROUNDING VALUE field, a multiple of this value is always used in the purchase order.

Material requirements planning view 2

In MATERIAL REQUIREMENTS PLANNING VIEW 2, you can define further parameters for the material requirements planning (see Figure 4.7.

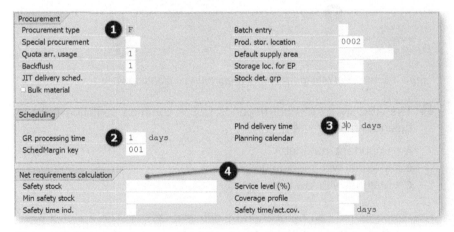

Figure 4.7: Material master: material requirements planning view 2

❶ Here, the entry in the PROCUREMENT TYPE field indicates the type of procurement on which the material is based. This can be external procurement (F)—that is, procurement from a vendor or another plant—in-house production (E), or both types of procurement (X). If there is no entry in this field, there is no procurement.

❷ You can enter a value in the GR PROCESSING TIME field even if there is no automated procurement. In this case, the processing time is calculated using the planned delivery time and also taken into account in a vendor rating.

❸ When you create purchasing info records, the value from the material master is entered in the PLND DELIVERY TIME field. In the same way, when purchase requisitions are created, the delivery date is calculated based on the defined planned delivery time.

❹ In this area, you can define parameters that support system-based procurement.

I will not address the MATERIAL REQUIREMENTS PLANNING VIEWS 3 and 4 in this book as they are used on a very company-specific basis. They are not relevant for the procurement transaction described here.

4.2   The purchasing info record

The *purchasing info record* contains all of the information required for purchasing for a material, service, or for goods that you procure from a vendor. In contrast to the material master, in the purchasing info record there is a unique assignment of the procurement goods to the procurement source. When the corresponding material is ordered, data from the purchasing info record is entered in the purchase order form by default.

If you want to create a purchasing info record, you can access the corresponding initial screen (see Figure 4.8) via the following path: LOGISTICS • MATERIALS MANAGEMENT • PURCHASING • MASTER DATA • INFO RECORD • CREATE. Alternatively, you can use transaction ME11.

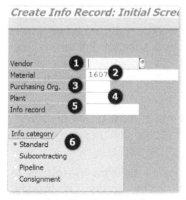

Figure 4.8: Creating an info record: initial screen

To create the info record, you have to enter information in the following fields:

❶ In the VENDOR field, enter the vendor number from the SAP system.

❷ In the MATERIAL field, enter the material number of the material you want to procure from this vendor.

❸ In the PURCHASING ORG. field, enter the unit in the company for which the material entered under ❷ is to be procured. The purchasing organization used here must match the purchasing organization for which the vendor was created.

❹ PLANT: within the purchasing organization there may be various plants for which the material is to be procured. If you do not enter a value in this field, the purchasing info record is created on a cross-plant basis so that other plants can access it as well. How you proceed depends on how your company is organized, for example.

❺ INFO RECORD: if you assign the info record number manually, you could enter a corresponding number here. If, instead of searching for an info record you want to change (transaction ME12) or look at (transaction ME13) an info record, you can do that by entering the info record number. In this case, the details in fields 1–3 are not necessary.

❻ The entry selected under INFO CATEGORY indicates which ordering process you want to use:

▶ STANDARD: in this ordering process, a standard purchase order is created which is subject to no requirements other than those legally required (price, quantity, etc.). An example is a purchase order for office materials.

▶ SUBCONTRACTING: if you provide a vendor with materials which they finish off and then return, this is a subcontracting process. The price defined in the purchasing info record contains only the finishing costs. One example of this is the painting of metal parts which you manufacture yourself.

▶ PIPELINE: in this case, you procure material (e. g., oil or power) via a (pipe)line. The purchasing info record contains the removal prices.

▶ CONSIGNMENT: in this case, the supplier delivers the goods to your warehouse but is still the owner of the goods. The transfer of ownership takes place when the customer takes the goods from the warehouse.

You do not have to enter information in fields ❹ and ❺.

As soon as you have entered or selected the corresponding data for your situation, the GENERAL DATA screen appears for you to enter information (see Figure 4.9).

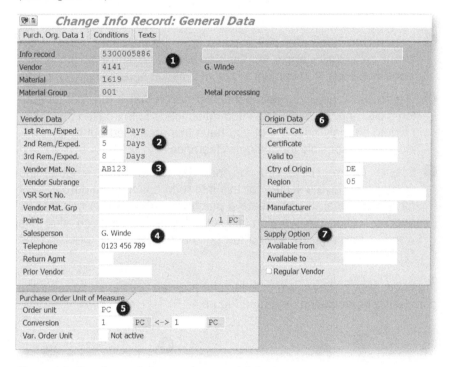

Figure 4.9: Creating an info record: general data

❶ This area contains the header information and the fields are filled from the vendor master or from the material master record. This information is also shown on the subsequent screens and you cannot change it. However, if you work in multiple SAP sessions in parallel, you can always check which info record you are currently making changes for.

❷ REM./EXPED.: in these fields you determine the frequency with which a reminder is to be sent to a vendor when no order acknowledgment exists in the system.

❸ Under VENDOR MAT. NO., you enter the material designation that the vendor uses. This entry helps you to avoid misunderstandings and makes it easier for the vendor to assign your purchase order to his own range.

❹ The entries in the SALESPERSON and TELEPHONE fields are taken from the vendor master, provided you have entered this information there. If no data is defined in the vendor master or if this information is not valid for the material that you want to create the purchasing info record for, you can enter the relevant information here.

❺ ORDER UNIT: the order unit is taken from the material master. If different order units apply for this vendor, for example packages instead of pieces, you can enter this information here.

❻ ORIGIN DATA: here you define the information that is relevant for customs clearing. Because this information leads to tax-based payables, I would strongly advise that you have this area filled out by the employees responsible for customs clearance.

❼ SUPPLY OPTION: here you can indicate, for example, whether the vendor you have selected for this info record is the standard vendor for this material. If you create a purchase order for this material for another vendor, a warning message appears. You can skip this warning message by saving the purchase order or by pressing the Enter key.

Press the Enter key again or select the next tab Purch. Org. Data 1 to enter the purchasing organization data (see Figure 4.10).

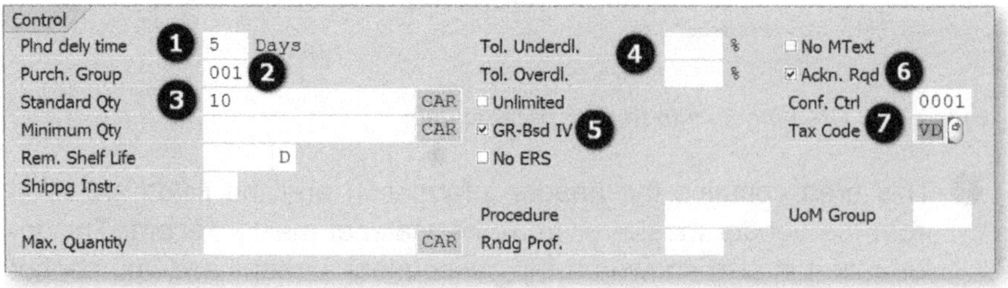

Figure 4.10: Info record purchasing organization data: control data

❶ PLND DELY TIME: if the planned delivery time for the vendor used here deviates from the time defined in the material master, you can enter this here.

94

❷ PURCH. GROUP: this information is also taken from the material master and you can change it if necessary.

❸ The STANDARD QTY and MINIMUM QTY fields influence the purchase requisitions created during material requirements planning for the materials for this vendor. By entering minimum quantities, you can avoid surcharges for below-minimum order quantities, for example.

❹ By specifying tolerances for under and overdelivery, on one hand you safeguard the material availability if you do not accept any underdeliveries; on the other hand, by limiting overdelivery, you can prevent goods receipts being posted without consultation if the vendor exceeds the tolerance you specify for overdelivery. This allows you to regulate the volume kept in the warehouse and for materials which are subject to aging, avoids items being thrown away.

❺ GR-BSD IV: click this checkbox to activate or deactivate the goods receipt-based invoice verification.

❻ ACKN. RQD: activating this checkbox is a prerequisite for being able to send reminders. You define the type of acknowledgment or confirmation you expect in the CONF. CTRL field (see Figure 4.11).

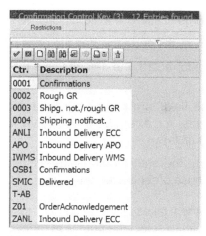

Figure 4.11: Info record confirmation control key

❼ TAX CODE: when selecting the tax code, just like for the origin data in the general data part, you should consult with the customs department as the entry here also leads to a tax-based payable. The tax code is also used if you have agreed to the credit memo procedure

with the vendor. Because your company issues the tax-based relevant document in this case, you must avoid errors in this area.

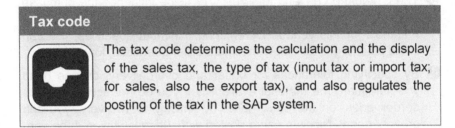

Tax code

The tax code determines the calculation and the display
of the sales tax, the type of tax (input tax or import tax;
for sales, also the export tax), and also regulates the
posting of the tax in the SAP system.

Under PURCH. ORG. DATA 1, you also have to define the conditions (see
Figure 4.12).

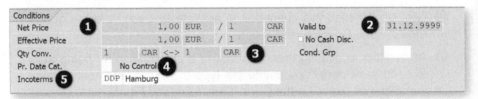

Figure 4.12: Info record purchasing organization data: conditions

❶ NET PRICE: here you enter the price, the currency, and the price unit.

❷ VALID TO: when you create the info record, the default value for this
date is **12/31/9999**.

❸ QTY CONV.: the values for these fields are taken from the material
master. You can use these fields, for example, if you have fixed
packaging units (e. g., always 20 units).

❹ PR. DATE CAT. (see Figure 4.13): the entry in this field defines the
price that is used when the purchase order is created.

The *pricing* in the purchase order then takes place according to your
selection. For example, it can be useful to select the purchase order date
for materials that are subject to daily prices or if, within the delivery time,
a new price becomes valid due to a change of fiscal year or current negotiations with the vendor.

Pricing Date Co	Short Descript.
	No Control
1	Purchase Order Date
2	Delivery Date
3	Current Date
4	Manual
5	GR Date

Figure 4.13: Info record conditions: pricing date type

The *pricing date type* is also determined by the Incoterms. Hence, differentiating between the delivery date and the goods receipt date makes sense if the delivery is not made by the vendor, as is the case for "ex works" deliveries, for example.

You also have to agree the type you select with the vendor to avoid having to clarify invoices later.

❺ INCOTERMS: the value for this field is taken from the material master. If the terms of delivery are different for your vendor, you can enter them here.

In principle, you can end the creation of the purchasing info record here by clicking 🖫. However, I would recommend at least entering the validity of the price according to the quotation or the agreement with the vendor. Click Conditions to access the following view (Figure 4.14):

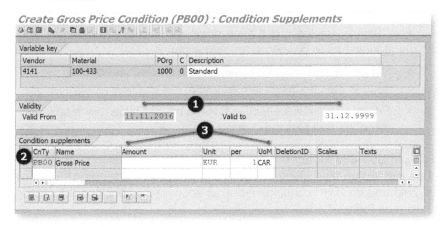

Figure 4.14: Info record: creating new conditions

① VALIDITY: enter the period for which the price is valid.

② CNTY (condition type): the value in this field specifies which price elements are to be used for pricing. In addition to the material price, there are freight charges, taxes, or surcharges and discounts, for example.

③ In the AMOUNT, UNIT, PER, and UoM columns, you can enter the price, the currency unit, the quantity per unit of measure, and the unit of measure.

Price validity

 Even if it can be very convenient to leave the price validity as 12/31/9999, this setting has business consequences for the company. The creation or addition of new conditions can mean that an old condition remains valid (until 12/31/9999). It is not used for pricing but must be included in the inventory valuation in accordance with the *lowest value principle* because in the future, the material can allegedly be procured at a different price.

Evaluations at the info record level also become more difficult or even impossible due to the condition not being maintained.

The SAP system generally differentiates between three types of price:

▶ *Gross price*: the gross price does not take any surcharges and deductions (e. g., discounts) into account.

▶ *Net price*: the net price takes all surcharges and deductions defined in the conditions into account.

▶ *Effective price*: the effective price is the net price minus any cash discount, and plus the delivery costs.

You can also add further condition types to the gross price. You can access a selection by clicking the white boxes ☐ next to the first highlighted field under CTYP (condition type) as soon as you position the cursor there (see Figure 4.15).

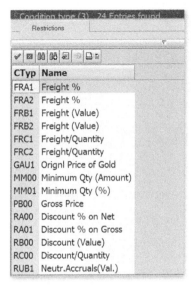

Figure 4.15: Creating info records: condition types

There is a basic differentiation between quantity-specific or weight-specific and fixed and percentage-based conditions.

Quantity-specific or weight-specific conditions, such as **FRC1 Freight/quantity** or **RC00 Discount/quantity**, are applied if the costs and discounts expected increase with the purchase order quantity. For example, if a vendor grants 1% discount for an order of 1,000 pieces, 2% discount for a quantity of 2,000 pieces, etc., you can define these conditions in a scale.

A **fixed** amount arises, for example, if EUR 20 customs duty is due per delivery = **ZOB1,** or a vendor charges processing costs per purchase order = **ZB00**.

If the surcharges or deductions are dependent on the delivery value, use a *percentage-based* condition. For example, **FRA1 = 3%** means that the calculated freight costs of 3% of the net price x quantity = net purchase order value. The same applies to percentage-based discounts **RA00**: the agreed discount value is calculated on the net order value.

Whether and how conditions are used in your company depends on the type of business, the organizational structure, and business considerations.

Double-click the condition to create the scale prices (see Figure 4.16).

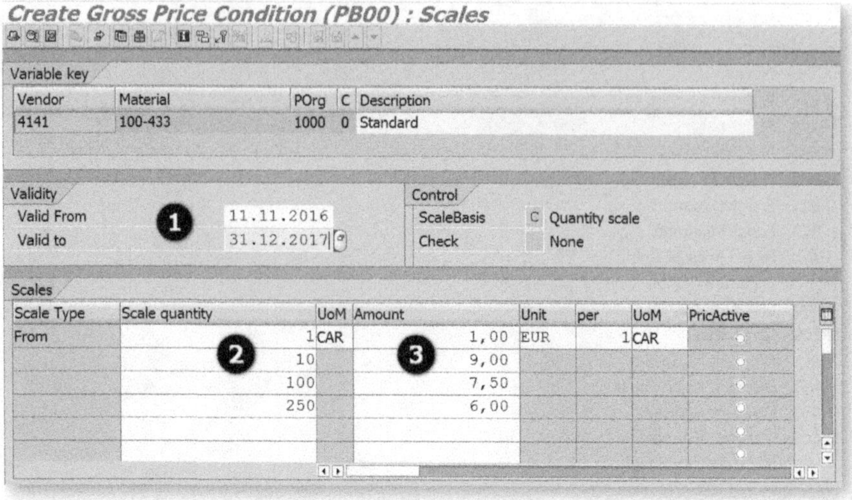

Figure 4.16: Info record conditions: creating scales

❶ VALIDITY: here, you enter the period for which a price is valid; alternatively, you leave the default values taken from the condition.

❷ SCALE QUANTITY: the value in this field specifies the purchase order quantity from which the price displayed under ❸ is valid.

You can now save the info record. The message PURCHASING INFO RECORD 5300005886 1000 WAS ADDED then appears.

If you want to add new conditions to an existing info record, select transaction ME12 or follow the path: LOGISTICS • MATERIALS MANAGEMENT • PURCHASING • MASTER DATA • INFO RECORD • CHANGE.

Click Conditions to display the view shown in Figure 4.17.

By double-clicking a condition or highlighting it and clicking ✔ Choose , you can open the condition.

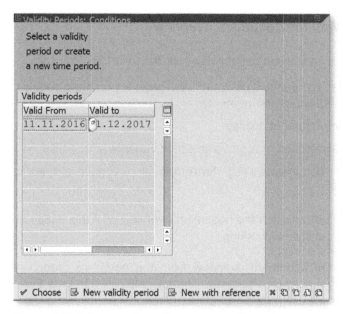

Figure 4.17: Info record: creating new conditions

You define a new validity period by clicking the icon of the same name or using a reference [New with reference]. It makes sense to use a reference in particular if you have defined price scales or use many different conditions for pricing. This allows you to reduce the effort involved in price maintenance.

Price maintenance in the info record

SAP also offers a mass change function for info records. You can use this function for both the general data and the purchasing organization data. However, you can only preselect useful purchasing info records to be changed if the relevant data has been maintained. Consult your system administrator.

4.3   Working with the document overview

In the *document overview* you can display your daily worklist. You can:

- ▶ Select the document type (purchase orders, purchase requisitions, scheduling agreements, etc.)
- ▶ Define the document display
- ▶ Adjust the selection or remove selection variants
- ▶ Search for documents, (e. g., for a material, a vendor, a specific date, etc.)

Of course, you can also switch the document overview off if this does not fit your own personal style of working.

You can access the document overview from the purchase order via transactions ME21N (CREATE PURCHASE ORDER), ME22N (CHANGE PURCHASE ORDER), or ME23N (VIEW PURCHASE ORDER). The following view appears (see Figure 4.18):

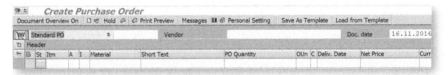

Figure 4.18: Document overview: purchase order view

Click ⌷ Document Overview On to open the document overview (see Figure 4.19).

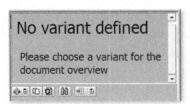

Figure 4.19: Document overview switched on

Click the selection icon ✧ ◢ to open the list of possible documents which you can select from (see Figure 4.20).

Figure 4.20: Document overview: variants

Now select the documents you want to process. In our example, double-click **Purchase Requisitions**.

A window opens in which you can define the criteria for your selection. There is a differentiation between GENERAL SELECTIONS (see Figure 4.21) and PROGRAM SELECTIONS (see Figure 4.22).

Figure 4.21: Document overview: general selections

Under GENERAL SELECTIONS, you can select whether you want to display OPEN ONLY purchase requisitions, that is, those for which no further action has been taken yet. This can be helpful for determining the purchase requisitions for which the release process has not yet been performed or was stopped for certain reasons. You can also display RELEASED ONLY purchase requisitions in order to assign a source of supply, for example. If you select ASSIGNED, OPEN, AND RELEASED, you determine the purchase requisitions that you can convert into a purchase order directly.

MAX. NO. OF HITS: the default value in this field is **5000**. Of course, it is helpful to set this value high if there are actually a large number of purchase requisitions to be processed, they are then all displayed.

Under PROGRAM SELECTIONS, you can refine the selection (see Figure 4.22).

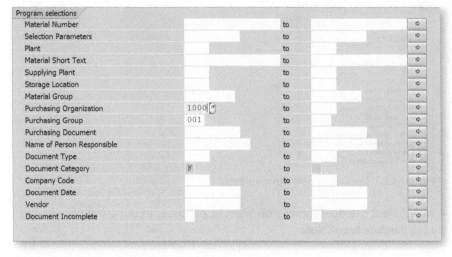

Figure 4.22: Document overview: program selections

Here it makes sense to enter a value in the PURCHASING GROUP field. You should also enter information in the PURCHASING ORGANIZATION and DOCUMENT DATE fields. Just like other selection variables, you can either enter an individual date or select a period by entering a value in the To field. This selection should suffice for displaying the purchase requisitions for which you are responsible.

All other selection options should be used on a case by case basis—for example, if you want to call up all purchase requisitions for a material due to bottlenecks or for a vendor for the purpose of price negotiations.

To avoid having to reselect your standard values every day, you can save them as a *variant*. In the toolbar, choose GOTO • VARIANTS • SAVE AS VARIANT (see Figure 4.23).

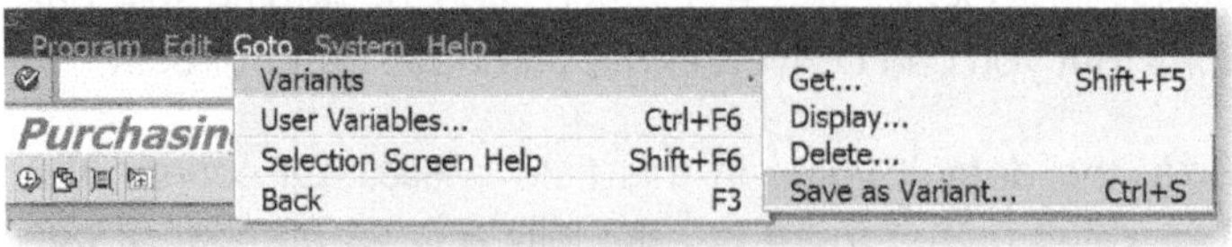

Figure 4.23: Saving a selection as a variant

The VARIANT ATTRIBUTES screen then appears (see Figure 4.24).

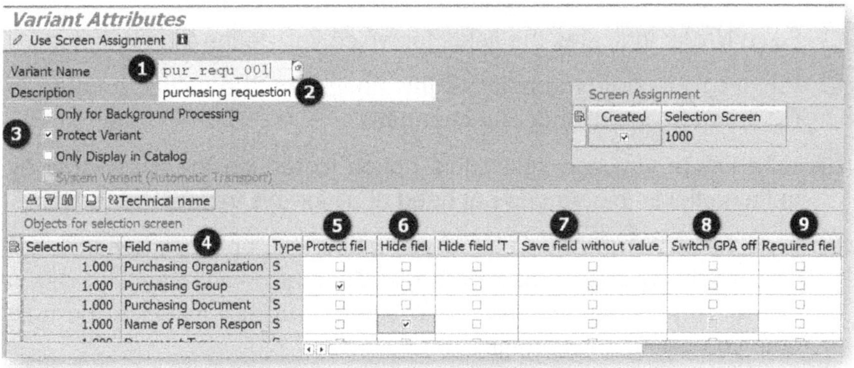

Figure 4.24: Document overview: variant attributes

Here you assign certain properties to your variant. The list shown is not complete. You can display further attributes and define them according to your needs. In the following, I will address some of the attributes by way of example and explain the general function of this overview.

❶ In the VARIANT NAME field, enter a name that is as expressive as possible. Unfortunately, there is a character limit in this field; nevertheless, you can still enter an expressive name if, for example, conventions have been defined.

❷ Under DESCRIPTION, you can add information for this variant. This should be a more extensive explanation about what can be selected using this variant.

❸ In this area, you can select the ONLY FOR BACKGROUND PROCESSING checkbox for the variant, which then means that the variant cannot be opened in dialog mode. By selecting this checkbox you reduce the load on the server, particularly for very extensive evaluations.

If you select PROTECT VARIANT, the variant can be executed by other users but not changed. If you intend to use this variant frequently, you should activate this option when you create the variant to prevent accidental changes.

Selecting the ONLY DISPLAY IN CATALOG option means that this variant is displayed only in the variant catalog. If you display the variants by pressing the **F4** key in a value list, this variant does not appear. You can use this function to separate frequently used variants from rarely used variants and thus maintain a more clearly arranged value list.

❹ FIELD NAME: indicates the fields for which you define the attributes.

❺ PROTECT FIELD: if you activate this checkbox, the values entered in the variant can no longer be changed.

❻ HIDE FIELD: you can select this option to reduce the list overall by defining fields that you do not need at all for this variant.

❼ SAVE FIELD WITHOUT VALUES: if you select this option, when you call up the variant, any entries already defined are not overwritten with a space. Any values that you have entered are still included the next time you call up the variant.

❽ SWITCH GPA OFF: activating this option means that existing initial values are not entered in the selection fields. This function is not available for all fields because initial values do not exist for every field.

❾ REQUIRED FIELD: fields with this option selected must contain an entry. If you use a lot of variants, this makes processing faster.

Adopt your settings by clicking `⌀ Use Screen Assignment`. Then click 🖫 to save your variant

Variant names

 When you create the variants, it makes sense to define conventions for the names. This ensures that if a colleague is unexpectedly unavailable, you can still find and use his variants easily.

The next time you call up the document overview and click GET VARIANT 🖼 in the overview, another view is displayed (see Figure 4.25.

To keep the results list manageable, it makes sense to enter a value in at least one of the search fields. Which search field will be most useful depends, among other things, on whether you have assigned *naming conventions* in your company, for example. In our example (see Figure 4.26), we have entered a value in the CREATED BY search field.

Find Variant		
Variant		⇨
Environment		⇨
Created By	JOST	⇨
Changed By		⇨
Original Language		⇨

⊕ ✖

Figure 4.25: Finding variants

ABAP: Variant Directory of Program AQZZ/SAPQUERY/MEMEPO==========

⊟ ⊽ 卌 ⊞ ▭

Variant Catalog for Program AQZZ/SAPQUERY/MEMEPO===========

Variant name	Short Description	Environme	Protecte	Created By	Created On	Changed By	Last Changed O
PUR_REQU_001	purchasing requestion	A	X	JOST	16.11.2016		
VENDOR	41xx	A	X	JOST	16.11.2016		

Figure 4.26: Finding variants: result

Double-click the desired variant to open it.

You can also create variants in many other programs, which can make your daily work easier.

Variants with variable attributes

 To call up a regular (e. g., weekly or monthly) evaluation using a variant, it is helpful to define a variable date calculation in the variant. You can do this via transaction SE38 in the variant maintenance. The authorization for this transaction is usually only assigned to the system administration. Contact your key user and ask for support.

4.3.1 Personal settings in purchase orders

When you call up transactions ME21N to ME23N, via the ⊞ Personal Setting icon you can access an area in which you define settings which are valid exclusively for your user ID and are therefore defaulted when you create purchase orders (see Figure 4.27).

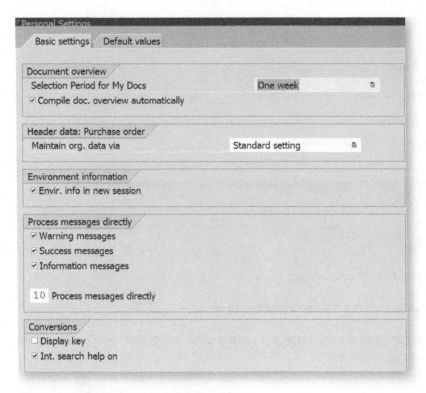

Figure 4.27: Personal settings: basic settings

Here, on the BASIC SETTINGS tab, you can define the period for which you want your own documents to be displayed in the document overview. This is certainly useful because a large number of documents are created during your daily work. If all of these were to be displayed, the list would no longer be clear and manageable and any work relief would be lost.

If you select that the organizational data is to be maintained via **Standard Settings**, you can define the basic settings on the DEFAULT VALUES tab (see Figure 4.28).

Click [More Fields ...] to expand the selection and increase the number of default values to meet your requirements (see Figure 4.29).

108

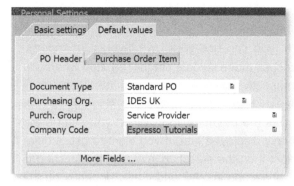

Figure 4.28: Personal settings: default values

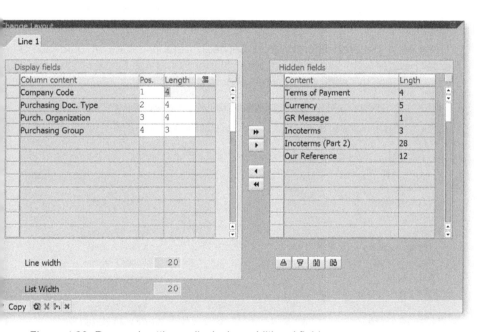

Figure 4.29: Personal settings: displaying additional fields

You can add all of the fields required from the right-hand box to the standard display on the left by clicking ◀ . If you want to remove parameters from the standard display, proceed in the opposite direction ▶ . If you want to add or remove all of the entries from the list, select either ◀◀ or ▶▶ accordingly.

Confirm your selection by pressing the [Enter] key or by clicking ✔ Copy .

Using your own layouts

 In principle, you can use your own layouts for reports. You can access these layouts via the ▦ icon when you use the respective transaction. Using the SETTINGS • LAYOUT MANAGEMENT function, you can also define your own layout as the default layout. When you call up the report, this layout is always displayed first. If you want to use a different layout, you can select it on the selection screen. This function is not provided for every transaction in SAP and it also depends on the general settings. Hence, if you cannot find this option, it is probably not offered by your SAP system.

There is a general differentiation between default values at purchase order header level and line item level. Under PURCHASE ORDER ITEM, you can configure the settings shown in Figure 4.30.

Personal Settings		
Basic settings	Default values	
PO Header	Purchase Order Item	
Item category	Standard	☐ Always Propose
Acct assignment cat.		☐ Always Propose
Delivery Date		
Plant	1000	☑ Always Propose
Storage Location		☐ Always Propose
Material Group		☐ Always Propose
Requisitioner		☐ Always Propose
Req. Tracking Number		☐ Always Propose
Promotion		☐ Always Propose
☑ Acknowledgment Reqd		☑ Always Propose
More Fields ...		

Figure 4.30: Personal settings: default values at line item level

Here too, the default settings you should define are dependent on your daily business and the organizational structure of the purchasing functions.

110

Acknowledgement required

Irrespective of the organizational circumstances, I recommend that you always select ACKNOWLEDGMENT REQUIRED.

4.4 Creating favorites

4.4.1 Favorites for SAP transactions

In order to access the transactions that you use frequently in your every-day work more quickly, I recommend that you create *favorites*.

Figure 4.31 shows the selection of the subitem FAVORITES in the SAP EASY ACCESS menu:

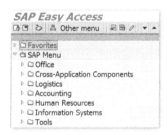

Figure 4.31: Creating favorites: access via the menu

Once you have selected FAVORITES, right-click the mouse. The view shown in Figure 4.32 appears.

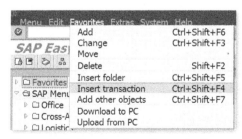

Figure 4.32: Creating favorites: selection

111

Confirm the selection INSERT TRANSACTION by clicking with the mouse.

In the next window, you can enter the transaction code (see Figure 4.33):

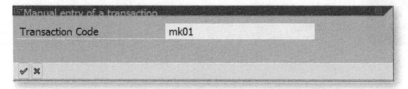

Figure 4.33: Creating favorites: entering the transaction code

Confirm the entry by pressing **Enter** or by clicking ✔. The transaction then appears in the FAVORITES list with a short description (see Figure 4.34).

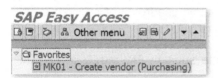

Figure 4.34: Creating favorites: transaction inserted

There will be a number of transactions that you use frequently during your work with the SAP system. Therefore, I strongly recommend that you create a folder structure (see Figure 4.35). To do this, select FAVOR-ITES and then INSERT FOLDER from the menu bar.

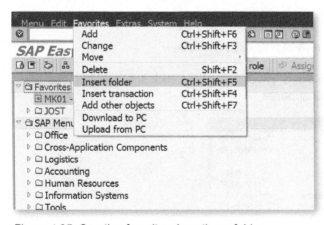

Figure 4.35: Creating favorites: inserting a folder

You then give the folder a name (see Figure 4.36), and you can add further transactions at this folder level.

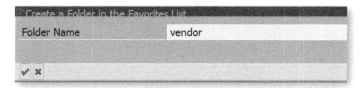

Figure 4.36: Creating favorites: entering the name of the folder

By way of example, Figure 4.37 shows a folder structure which can be helpful in the procurement process.

Figure 4.37: Creating favorites: folder structure

4.4.2 Favorites for other links

You can also create favorites for other documents or Internet links as well as SAP transactions. To do this, insert a new folder in the structure to give a clearer overview. Of course, you can also assign the links to the existing structure if you wish to do so.

As shown in Figure 4.38, choose FAVORITES and then ADD OTHER OB-JECTS from the menu bar .In the window that appears (see Figure 4.38), you can define the type of object concerned.

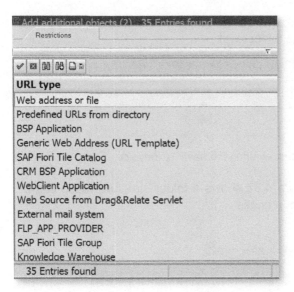

Figure 4.38: Creating favorites: selecting other objects

You can now link directly to Internet or intranet pages. This is helpful if you want to access catalogs for selection in the Internet, or to find regulations and instructions in the intranet.

A dialog box appears. Here you can enter the name and the address for the link (see Figure 4.39).

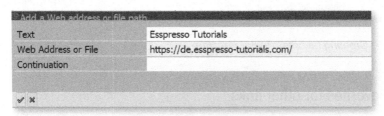

Figure 4.39: Other objects: creating the web address

Confirm your entries with the ⌈Enter⌉ key or by clicking ✅ .

The new link is now displayed in the updated favorites view (see Figure 4.40).

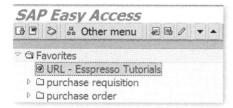

Figure 4.40: Creating favorites: Internet link inserted

By double-clicking the favorite (here URL - ESPRESSO TUTORIALS), you can access the associated Internet page (see Figure 4.41).

Figure 4.41: Accessing the Internet from the SAP favorites

4.4.3 Downloading and uploading favorites

To make your own favorites available to other users or to use them yourself for different systems, you can upload them to your personal computer. To do this, choose FAVORITES • DOWNLOAD TO PC (see Figure 4.35).

Now select a storage location (see Figure 4.42). In the standard system, SAP suggests the storage location which was created on your computer when the program was installed. However, just like for all other files, you can select a different storage location via Windows Explorer if you wish.

Figure 4.42: Creating favorites: downloading favorites to a storage location

General favorites structure

 With the exception of standard transactions, in many ways the way you work in an SAP system depends on your own style of working or on how much your colleagues like to experiment.

If you save the favorites to a central drive, you can enable all colleagues assigned to a function or an organizational area to access the frequently used transactions. These transactions can then be presented and the working method explained as part of a general information event. This ensures a continual improvement process.

If you save the favorites as a text file (file ending in .txt), you ensure that all colleagues can open this file without any conversion problems.

If you want to add a further system—for example, a test system or the work center for a new employee—you can add the favorites to the new system under the FAVORITES menu item by selecting UPLOAD FROM PC (see Figure 4.35). In the same way as for a download, when you select this menu item, the Windows Explorer view appears and you can select the relevant file.

4.5   Helpful evaluation functions

I use the following two functions if I have to answer queries from vendors, for example, or if I want to display purchase orders or goods receipts for a specific vendor, material, or period.

4.5.1   Purchase order list displays

You can use the info record list displays to determine which vendors have already been assigned for a material or which range of materials is purchased from a specific vendor.

In addition to the display function, the PURCHASE ORDER LIST DISPLAYS function also allows you to navigate directly to the purchase order. This can be very convenient if you have to change several purchase orders or you need an overview of the purchase orders for which prices, price units, currencies, or etc., have to be changed, for example.

List displays are also a useful aid if you do not have authorization for the SAP QuickViewer or little to no experience in working with this tool.

By way of example, I will explain the use of the list display BY VENDOR (see Figure 4.43). However, you can also trigger the display with other parameters, such as material groups, the supplying plant, etc.

▽ 🗁 List Displays
    🔹 ME2L - By Vendor
    🔹 ME2M - By Material
    ▷ 🗀 By Account Assignment
    🔹 ME2C - By Material Group
    🔹 ME2B - By Tracking Number
    🔹 ME2N - By PO Number
    🔹 ME2W - By Supplying Plant
    🔹 MELB - Transactions per Tracking Number

Figure 4.43: List displays for purchase orders: selecting the list criteria

If your task is part of a project, you should use transaction ME2J instead. In this transaction, you can display your purchase orders on a project-specific basis (see Figure 4.44).

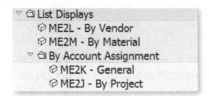

Figure 4.44: List displays: purchase orders for a project

Via the following path, you can access the LIST DISPLAYS: PURCHASE ORDERS FOR VENDOR function: LOGISTICS • MATERIALS MANAGEMENT • PURCHASING • PURCHASE ORDER • LIST DISPLAYS • BY VENDOR. Alternatively, you can call up transaction ME2L directly. The overview of selection criteria as shown in Figure 4.45 then appears. These criteria help you to restrict the range to be used for the search. By entering the various selection criteria, you can also restrict the search results to your requirements. The default entry for the scope of the list is always BEST (for purchase orders).

Purchasing Documents per Vendor
Choose...

Vendor	❶	to	⇨
Purchasing Organization	❷	to	⇨
Scope of List	BEST		
Selection Parameters		to	⇨
Document Type		to	⇨
Purchasing Group	❸	to	⇨
Plant	❹	to	⇨
Document Incomplete		to	⇨
Item Category		to	⇨
Account Assignment Category		to	⇨
Delivery Date		to	⇨
Validity Key Date			
Range of Coverage to			
Document Number		to	⇨
Material		to	⇨
Material Group		to	⇨
Document Date	❺	to ❻	⇨
Intern. Article No. (EAN/UPC)		to	⇨
Vendor's Material Number		to	⇨
Vendor Subrange		to	⇨

Figure 4.45: Purchase order list display: selection

❶ Under VENDOR, you can enter either an individual vendor number or a number range. By clicking ⇨ , you can choose between the following options:

▶ Select Single Values : here you enter different purchase order numbers or insert them from a list.

▶ Select Ranges : if you select this option, you can select the purchase order numbers in a number range. All purchase orders with a number within this number range are then displayed.

▶ Exclude Single Values : this option is useful if, for example, you have previously defined a number range for the display but do not want to include individual purchase order numbers.

▶ Exclude Ranges : as well as selecting number ranges, you can also exclude them. If you want to exclude certain order types, use the wild card *: for example, if you enter 45*, no standard purchase orders are displayed.
However, because you can also use this selection for all other selection options, it is possible that number ranges in the area of the purchasing organization, material group, or material numbers will be excluded.

❷ Limiting the selection via the PURCHASING ORGANIZATION field can be useful if you create purchase orders for multiple organizational units or if there is a large number of purchasing organizations in your company. Limiting the display to certain values makes the results list clearer and easier to read.

❸ If you need the list display for your own work, it makes sense to enter the values created for you in the PURCHASING GROUP field. If multiple purchasing groups are assigned to you, you can also restrict the display to the data relevant for this evaluation here.

❹ Entering a value in the PLANT field has the same effect as the selection for the purchasing organization.

❺ I recommend that you always restrict the display via the DOCUMENT DATE field; in this view, this corresponds to the purchase order date. You can enter either a specific date or a period ❻.

4.5.2   Search with restricted information

I will now show you how to search for a vendor number if you only know the vendor name. You can also use the process described below in all other transactions which have the corresponding icon. It is also not limited solely to vendors; it applies in the same way for all other database information, such as material numbers.

When you click ⬛ (see Figure 4.45), the window shown in Figure 4.46 appears.

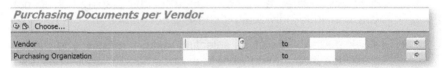

Figure 4.46: Purchase order list display: vendor search

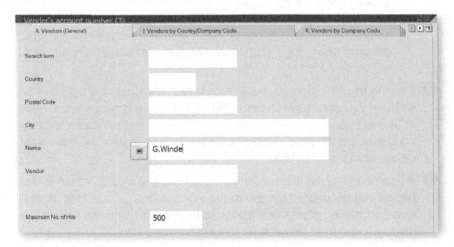

Figure 4.47: Purchase order list displays: vendor search by name

In the corresponding fields, enter the term you want to search for (see Figure 4.47). In the example shown, we are looking for the vendor **G. Winde**. You can now enter the search term in the corresponding fields. The search works by comparing strings, i.e., the system searches for exactly the term that you entered. It takes into account upper and lower case, special characters, and blanks. This is a clear example of how important it is to define naming conventions and—even more important—that everybody observes them.

Press **Enter** to display the search results (see Figure 4.48). By double-clicking the name of the vendor you are looking for, you can transfer this name to the selection screen.

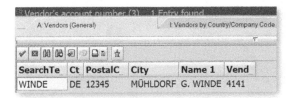

Figure 4.48: Purchase order list display: vendor search results

You can, of course, also search exclusively for documents for a specific material by not entering a vendor number. Now start the search by clicking EXECUTE.

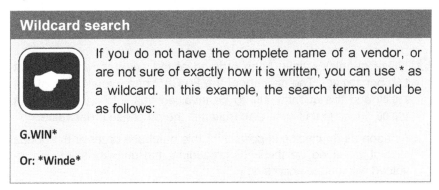

Wildcard search

If you do not have the complete name of a vendor, or are not sure of exactly how it is written, you can use * as a wildcard. In this example, the search terms could be as follows:

G.WIN*

Or: ***Winde***

Figure 4.49 shows an example with the results for a selection by vendor and date.

➊ In the header area, the information from the purchase order header is displayed: the purchase order number **4500017300**, document type (**NB**), vendor number **4141** and name **G. Winde**, purchasing group **001**, and the purchase order date **09/05/2016**.

➋ In the item area, the item number **00010**, material number **1607**, and plant **1000** are displayed.

➌ Under, you can see the purchase order quantity **100 CAR**, the quantity still to be delivered **80 CAR** and the quantity still to be invoiced **100 CAR**.

Purchasing Documents per Vendor

🖳 📋 Print Preview 🔳 PO History 🔳 Changes 🔳 Delivery Schedule 🔳 Services

```
PO        Type Vendor     Name                              PGp Order Date
  Item   Material          Short Text                           Mat. Group
    D I A Plnt SLoc           ❶  Order Qty     Un   Net Price  Curr.   per Un

4500017300 NB    4141     G. Winde                          001 05.09.2016
  00010 1607 ❷            1607 screw                 ❹          001
    K 1000                           100  CAR          1,50 EUR     100 PC
    In stockkeeping unit        10.000  PC            0,02 EUR       1 PC
    Still to be delivered    ❸    80  CAR          120,00 EUR    80,00 % ❺
    Still to be invoiced          100  CAR          150,00 EUR   100,00 %
4500017302 NB    4141     G. Winde                          000 25.10.2016
  00010 1607              1607 screw                            001
    K 1000                            50  CAR          1,50 EUR     100 PC
    In stockkeeping unit         5.000  PC            0,02 EUR       1 PC
    Still to be delivered          40  CAR           60,00 EUR    80,00 %
    Still to be invoiced           50  CAR           75,00 EUR   100,00 %
4500017303 NB    4141     G. Winde                          001 27.10.2016
  00010 1607              1607 screw                            001
    K 1000                            50  CAR          1,50 EUR     100 PC
    In stockkeeping unit         5.000  PC            0,02 EUR       1 PC
    Still to be delivered          45  CAR           67,50 EUR    90,00 %
    Still to be invoiced           50  CAR           75,00 EUR   100,00 %
```

Figure 4.49: Purchase order list display: results

❹ These quantities have been ordered at the price shown under(**EUR 1.50** per **100 PC**). The delivery of the 80 CAR has a total value of **EUR 120.00** and the quantity still to be invoiced has a total value of **EUR 150.00**, which in this case also matches the purchase order value.

As soon as an invoice is posted for this purchase order or the goods receipt is settled via the ERS procedure, the quantity still to be invoiced will reduce accordingly.

❺ shows the open delivery quantity and the invoice quantity in percent. In this case, **80.00%** of the material still has to be delivered and **100.00%** invoiced.

Double-click the purchase order number to go to the corresponding purchase order (see Figure 4.50). Alternatively, you can also click 🖳 (DIS-PLAY DOCUMENT) as shown in Figure 4.49. It is important, however, to make sure you place the cursor on the desired purchase order number first.

By clicking DISPLAY/CHANGE 🖉, you can change to editing mode and make changes to the purchase order (Figure 4.51).

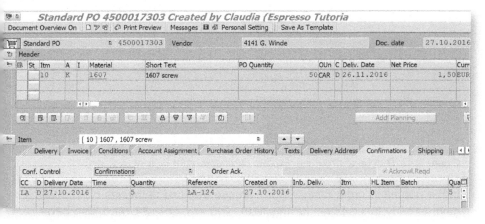

Figure 4.50: Purchase order list display: purchase order view

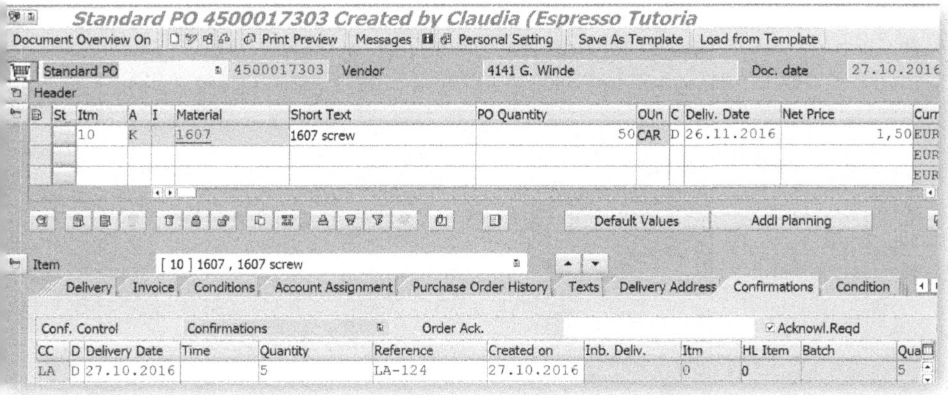

Figure 4.51: Purchase order list display: change purchase order

When you exit the purchase order view, either by saving or without making a change, you return to the results list of purchase orders and can process the next purchase order.

On the screen shown in Figure 4.49, place the cursor on an item in the list of purchasing documents and click 🗷 PO History to display detailed information (see Figure 4.52).

Order History for Purchase Order 4500017273 00010

GR/IR Assignment | Order Price Unit | Blocked Stock | Val. Blocked Stock

Cat.	Doc. no.	Itm	MvT	Pstg.dt.	Qty.in OUn		Value in local curr	
WE	5000020100	0001	101	20.08.15	50.000	PC	375,00	EUR
WE	5000020106	0001	101	21.10.15	50.000	PC	375,00	EUR
Total variances through IR							150,00-	EUR
Total goods receipts					100.000	PC	600,00	EUR
RE-L	5105608834	0001		02.11.15	50.000	PC	300,00	EUR
RE-L	5105608834	0002		02.11.15	50.000	PC	300,00	EUR
Total invoices					100.000	PC	600,00	EUR

Figure 4.52: Purchase order list display: purchase order history

In the purchase order history, you can see that two deliveries of type **WE** have already taken place for this item. Two invoices **RE-L** have also been entered for the item and two ERS settlements performed. Here too, you can double-click the document numbers to go to the view of the individual documents.

By clicking GR/IR Assignment , you can display an overview showing which invoices can be assigned to which purchase orders (see Figure 4.53).

Order History for Purchase Order 4500017273 00010

GR/IR Assignment | Order Price Unit | Blocked Stock | Val. Blocked Stock

Cat.	Doc. no.	Itm	MvT	Pstg.dt.	Qty.in OUn		Value in local curr	
Delivery Doc. 2015 5000020100 0001 123456								
WE	5000020100	0001	101	20.08.15	50.000	PC	375,00	EUR
Total variances through IR							75,00-	EUR
Total goods receipts					50.000	PC	300,00	EUR
RE-L	5105608834	0001		02.11.15	50.000	PC	300,00	EUR
Total invoices					50.000	PC	300,00	EUR
Delivery Doc. 2015 5000020106 0001								
WE	5000020106	0001	101	21.10.15	50.000	PC	375,00	EUR
Total variances through IR							75,00-	EUR
Total goods receipts					50.000	PC	300,00	EUR
RE-L	5105608834	0002		02.11.15	50.000	PC	300,00	EUR
Total invoices					50.000	PC	300,00	EUR

Figure 4.53: Purchase order list displays: GR/IR assignment

An internal invoice document **RE-L 5105608834** was assigned to delivery document **123456** from **08/20/2015** with goods receipt **WE**. This statement can be useful if any clarification is required with the vendor. In this view, you can also go to the original document by double-clicking the document number.

Click Blocked Stock to display the materials delivered for this purchase order and posted to the blocked stock.

Select an item in the list display and click 🗎 Changes to display an overview of all changes that have already been made for this item (see Figure 4.54).

Changes Purchase Order 4500017273 Item 10 ❶

Item	Object	Short text ❸	Action	New value	Old value	User	Date	Time
10	Confirmation 0001 ❷		Entered			JOST	20.10.2015	06:27:54
	Confirmation 0002		Entered			JOST	21.10.2015	06:58:25
	Item	Date of Price Determination	Changed	15.12.2015	26.10.2015	JOST	02.11.2015	10:49:29
		Effective value of item	Changed	1.500,00 EUR	1.125,00 EUR	JOST		10:47:35
		Gross order value in PO currency	Changed	1.500,00 EUR	1.125,00 EUR	JOST		
		Net Order Value in PO Currency	Changed	1.500,00 EUR	1.125,00 EUR	JOST		
		Net Price in Purchasing Document (i	Changed	0,60 EUR	0,75 EUR	JOST		
		Purchase Order Quantity	Changed	250.000 PC	150.000 PC	JOST		
		Purchasing Document Item Change	Changed	02.11.2015	19.10.2015	JOST		
	Schedule Line 0001	Item delivery date	Changed	03.11.2015	26.10.2015	JOST		10:49:29
		Scheduled Quantity	Changed	250.000 PC	150.000 PC	JOST		10:47:29
			Changed	100.000 PC	250.000 PC	JOST		10:49:29
		Statistics-Relevant Delivery Date	Changed	03.11.2015	26.10.2015	JOST		
	Schedule Line 0002		Entered			JOST		
	Schedule Line 0003		Entered			JOST		
	Schedule Line 0004		Entered			JOST		

Figure 4.54: Purchase order list display: changes to the purchase order item

The purchase order number and the item number are displayed in the header area of this view ❶.

In the OBJECT area ❷, you can see which element of the purchase order item was changed. In this case, both confirmations and schedule lines have been recorded and the item has also been changed.

The entry in the SHORT TEXT column ❸ provides further information about the type of change—for example, a change to the purchase order quantity, the scheduled quantity, etc. The entry in the ACTION column describes whether this is the first entry for the item or whether data that had already been entered and saved has been changed.

The information in columns ❹ and ❺ shows which new value was saved in the purchase order and which value was valid before the change, that is, the old value.

Columns ❻ (USER) and ❼ (DATE) also show who made the changes and when they made them.

Select a purchase order item in the list display and click ▣ Delivery Schedule to display the following overview (see Figure 4.55):

Delivery Schedule Purchase Ord 4500017273 00010

Deliv. Date	Time	Scheduled Qty	Qty Delivered	Quantity Issued	P
D 03.11.2015		100.000	100.000		R
D 15.11.2015		80.000	0		R
D 15.12.2015		20.000	0		R
D 31.12.2015		50.000	0		R
Total schedule lines		250.000	100.000		

Figure 4.55: Purchase order list displays: purchase order item delivery schedule

This table shows both the scheduled quantities defined in the purchase order and the quantities that have already been delivered.

You can also save the list display result as a file on your computer. To do this, choose SYSTEM • LIST • SAVE • LOCAL FILE from the menu bar. By selecting a corresponding checkbox you decide which format you want to save the list in (see Figure 4.56).

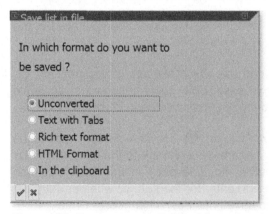

Figure 4.56: Purchase order list display: saving the list

If you select an unconverted list, as is the case in our example, the file is saved as a TXT file. Confirm your selection by clicking ✔.

You now have to define where the file should be saved and assign a name. Create a new file by clicking Generate (see Figure 4.57).

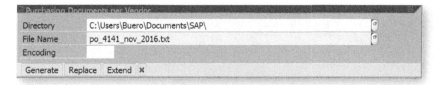

Figure 4.57: Purchase order list displays: storage location and file name

To call up the saved list, first open an Excel work folder and then the TXT file. You can now edit the list in Excel to get the desired statement. If you do not work with the Excel program on a daily basis and preparing the list appears to be very time-consuming due to the number of entries, I recommend that you contact a colleague from controlling. Controllers often have more extensive experience in preparing data and can help you with this task.

Creating ad-hoc evaluations

 Of course, this process is no replacement for a professional reporting tool. Nevertheless, it can still help you to get reliable evaluations for a vendor, material, or purchasing group quickly. You can, of course, save lists from the SAP system in many other applications.

Finally, I would like to show you which information is displayed if, in the PURCHASE ORDER list display (see Figure 4.45), you select the list scope ALL instead of BEST. This selection is very extensive (see Figure 4.58) and definitely only useful if you already know that you want to restrict the search to just a few purchase orders.

This very extensive selection provides you with all of the information available for the selected purchase order. You can also display this information by using the icons to select individual parameters in the list display. Therefore, I will only explain the individual areas briefly here.

Area ❶ contains the headings for the next columns. Further down (❷), the header information for the purchase order and the information for the purchase order item is listed as it is currently valid in the purchase order. You can also see the schedule lines here.

```
PO         Type Vendor    Name                            PGp Order Date
  Item  Material          Short Text                           Mat. Group
   D I A Plnt SLoc  ❶       Order Qty   Un     Net Price  Curr.   per Un
            SL Del. Date   Sched. Qty   Un

4500017302 NB   4141      G. Winde                        000 25.10.2016
  00010 1607             1607 screw                           001
        K 1000                          50  CAR  ❷      1,50  EUR    100 PC
      In stockkeeping unit           5.000  PC         0,02  EUR      1 PC
              D 26.10.2016             50  CAR PReq 10013813   00010
      Total goods receipts  ❸         10  CAR        15,00  EUR   20,00 %
      Still to be delivered           40  CAR        60,00  EUR   80,00 %
      Still to be invoiced            50  CAR        75,00  EUR  100,00 %
```

Cat.	Doc. no.	Itm	MvT	Pstg.dt.	Qty.in OUn	Value in local curr
WE	5000020104	0001	101	27.10.16	1 CAR	1,50 EUR
WE	5000020121	0001	101	08.11.16	❹ 9 CAR	13,50 EUR
Total goods receipts					10 CAR	15,00 EUR
BzWE	5000020104	0001		27.10.16	1 CAR	0,02 EUR
BzWE	5000020121	0001		08.11.16	9 CAR	0,14 EUR
Total delivery costs GR						0,16 EUR

```
Person Resp.       Date        Time      Transaction Change Document

Doc. Header 4500017302
Item     00010
JOST             27.10.2016 11.38.45 ME23N        671643
AEDAT      Purchasing Document Item Change Date Changed
Old: 25.10.2016
New: 27.10.2016
PRSDR        Price Printout Changed
Old: X      ❺
New:
SCHPR       Indicator: Estimated Price Changed
Old:
New: X
Confirmation 0001
JOST             27.10.2016 11.45.16 ME23N        671644
Entered
Confirmation 0002
JOST             27.10.2016 12.01.31 ME23N        671645
Entered
```

Figure 4.58: Purchase order list display: list scope ALL

The status of the purchase order fulfillment is shown under ❸. The precise breakdown of the goods and invoice receipts is shown under ❹. Under ❺, you can see all of the changes that have been made to this purchase order at header or line item level. Figure 4.58 shows merely an extract of the changes.

The list display is very useful for getting a quick overview and complete information for one or more purchase orders. Whether or not you integrate this list display in your work processes and how you do so depends on your personal method of working.

4.5.3   Displaying material documents

The list display for material documents is useful if you want to check goods receipts or search for individual delivery notes using the delivery note number. You can also use this function to track goods movements, e. g., internal transports or reversals of goods receipts.

You access the function via the following path: LOGISTICS • MATERIALS MANAGEMENT • INVENTORY MANAGEMENT • ENVIRONMENT • LIST DISPLAYS • MATERIAL DOCUMENTS. Alternatively, you can call up transaction MB51 directly.

In the same way as for the purchase order list display, you have to assign selection criteria for the material documents, as shown in Figure 4.59.

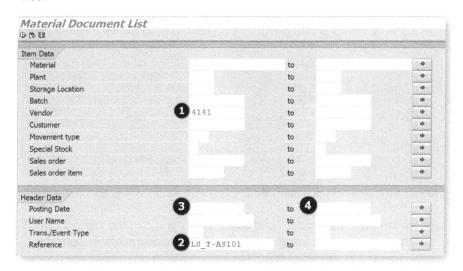

Figure 4.59: Material documents list display: selection criteria

In this example, we are searching for a delivery note. As you have to know the vendor, you can enter the vendor number in the VENDOR ❶ field. The entry of the delivery note number is also important = vendor REFERENCE ❷. If you know the date of the goods receipt posting, you can enter this under POSTING DATE ❸. If you know a period in which the goods receipt posting is supposed to have taken place, in the field TO ❹ you can enter a further date.

As a string comparison also takes place here, it is very important that the goods receipt employee enters delivery note numbers correctly.

Now start the search by clicking EXECUTE ⊕.

The following view shows the results of the search. All relevant information for the delivery note posting is displayed (see Figure 4.60).

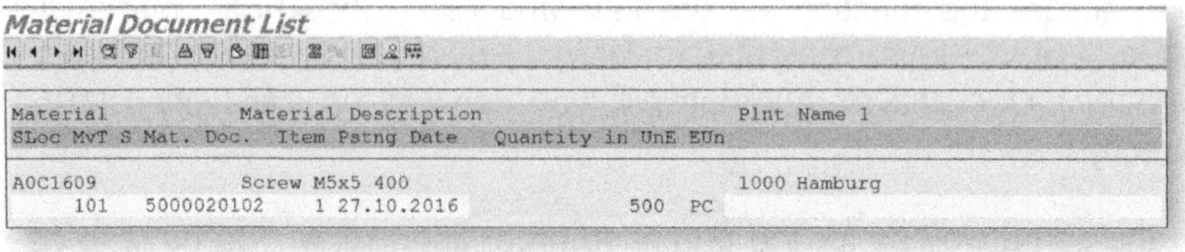

Figure 4.60: Material documents list display: navigation to the material document

By double-clicking the material document number, you can navigate to the material document (see Figure 4.61) and call up further information.

Figure 4.61: Material documents list display: material document 5000020102

As for the purchase order list display, when you exit the material document you return to the list and can view further documents if applicable.

4.5.4 Info record list displays

You can display a list for the purchasing info records (hereinafter referred to as info records). In the same way as for the purchase orders, you can call up the following info records:

▶ A material

▶ A vendor

► A material group

► Archived info records

► An order price history

► A quotation price history

Which variant you select depends on what information you require. If you want to know which vendors have already delivered a material, display the info records for the material. If, for example, you want to prepare for annual negotiations with a vendor, choose **Info Records per Vendor**. The option **For Material Group** can be useful if you want to check whether similar materials already exist in your material master—to bundle requirements, for example. The **Archived Info Records** option is available for info records that are no longer available in operational business. You can reactivate these records if you want to use a material, a certain vendor, or both again. The **Order Price History** and **Quotation Price History** options are self-explanatory. By way of example, I will explain the list display for purchasing info records for a vendor. Choose transaction ME1L or the following path: LOGISTICS • MATERIALS MANAGEMENT • PURCHASING • MASTER DATA • INFO RECORD • LIST DISPLAYS • FOR VENDOR.

The view shown in Figure 4.62 appears.

Under ❶, enter the number of the vendor whose info records you want to display.

If you are looking for a specific vendor material, it is helpful to enter a value in the VENDOR MATERIAL NUMBER field ❷. The prerequisite for entering this information is that the information has been maintained and the designation can be adopted 1:1 from the vendor.

I definitely recommend that you restrict the selection by entering a value in the PURCHASING ORGANIZATION field under ❸. This ensures that only info records that are valid for your area are displayed. Displaying info records for this vendor for other areas can be useful if you want to compare prices or search for related materials.

A value in the INFO CATEGORY field ❹ restricts the results list if you only want to display subcontracting info records, for example.

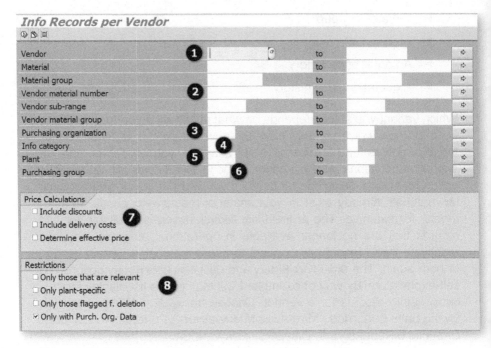

Figure 4.62: List display of info records for a vendor: selection

Whether or not an entry in the PLANT field ❺ is a useful restriction depends on the overall organization. In many companies, it is common to create info records on a cross-plant basis so that all plants can access the same prices.

Entering a value in the PURCHASING GROUP field ❻ supports the selection of your own materials but can also be helpful if the purchasing groups are set up according to material groups, for example.

Under ❼, you can decide how the price displayed is to be determined.

▶ If you select the INCLUDE DISCOUNTS option, the price displayed is reduced by the percentage rate that is valid once the first payment deadline has expired.

▶ If you select the INCLUDE DELIVERY COSTS option, this price component is also included in the price displayed.

▶ Select the DETERMINE EFFECTIVE PRICE option to include both cash discount amounts and delivery costs.

Under ❽, you activate the organizational restrictions.

▶ If you select ONLY THOSE THAT ARE RELEVANT, only info records that are valid for your plant are displayed.

▶ By choosing the ONLY PLANT-SPECIFIC option, you define that info records that have been created on a cross-plant basis are not displayed.

▶ You can also select the ONLY THOSE FLAGGED F. DELETION option to display data records as a worklist for data maintenance.

▶ If you select the ONLY WITH PURCH. ORG. DATA option, no results are displayed for info records to which no conditions have been assigned, for example.

In the results list for our example (see Figure 4.63), I have created a selection for the vendor and the purchasing organization. I have also selected the ONLY WITH PURCH. ORG. DATA option.

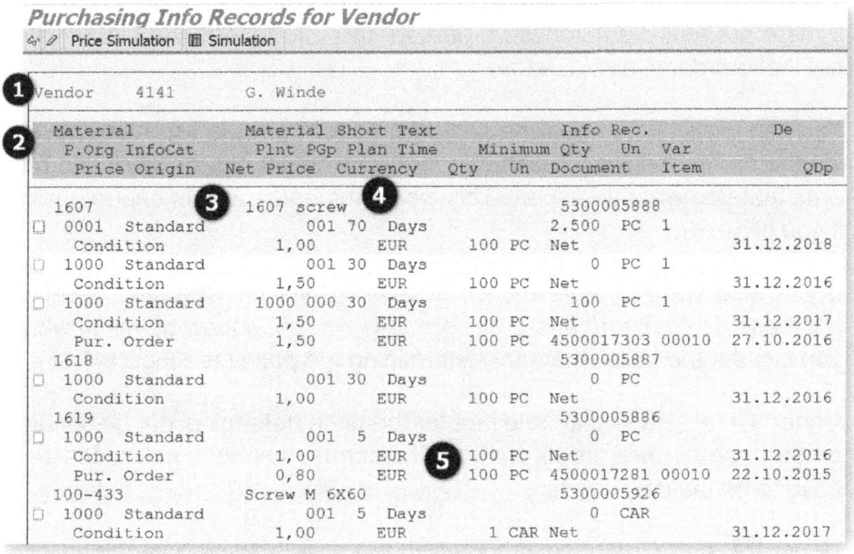

Figure 4.63: Info record list display: selection result

❶ shows the vendor for which the selection was executed. It shows the SAP vendor master number and the name of the vendor.

❷ provides explanations about how the column headings should be read. Unfortunately, the multi-line structure is not very clear but is a compromise to avoid the list being too wide.

❸ contains the information from the purchasing info record. With regard to ❹, unfortunately this is **not** the vendor's material number but rather the material text from the *material master*. If a material is procured from multiple vendors, the material master does not contain a vendor's material number. However, for an evaluation of info records for the purpose of assigning the material to be procured to the vendor uniquely, in my opinion it would be more useful if the vendor's material number or the manufacturer part number was displayed in the overview. This would make searches easier. This assignment would also help the vendor if you provide him with this list as part of price negotiations.

Under ❺, you can see that a purchase order with a reference to this info record has already been set up. The price, the purchase order quantity, and the purchase order number with purchase order date are displayed. If there are multiple purchase orders for this info record, the most recent purchase order is displayed.

You can click 🔍 to open the first info record from the list. Alternatively, via the corresponding checkboxes, you can select one or more info records that you want to display. This works the same way in change mode if you click ✏️.

If you also want to start a price simulation, via the checkbox select a purchasing info record and click Price Simulation. A window opens in which you can set the parameters for determining the price (see Figure 4.64).

Under ❶, enter the date relevant for the price determination. Depending on the type of pricing date and the Incoterms, this does not necessarily have to be the delivery date.

Under ❷, enter the quantity for which the price is to be determined, and under ❸, the quantity unit.

Under ❹, you decide which additional price elements are to be used to calculate the price. You can select the options INCL. CASH DISCOUNT and DELIVERY COSTS individually. If you select the EFFECTIVE PRICE option, both cost components are included in the price determination.

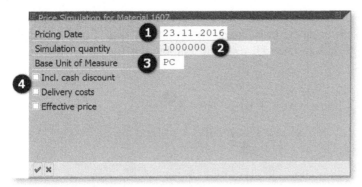

Figure 4.64: Info record list displays: price simulation parameters

Confirm your entries by clicking ✔. The following view appears (see Figure 4.65).

Purchasing Info Records for Vendor
✏ Price Simulation ▦ Simulation

```
Vendor      4141        G. Winde

 Material              Material Short Text                Info Rec.              De
   P.Org InfoCat         Plnt PGp Plan Time      Minimum Qty    Un  Var
     Price Origin      Net Price  Currency    Qty  Un  Document    Item              QDp

   1607               1607 screw                          5300005888
 □ 1000  Standard ①        001 30  Days                    0   PC  1
   -> Simulation          1,50       EUR       100 PC  Net
 □ 1000  Standard      1000 000 30  Days                  100   PC  1
   -> Simulation          1,50       EUR       100 PC  Net
     Pur. Order          1,50       EUR       100 PC  4500017303 00010  27.10.2016
   1618                                               5300005887
 □ 1000  Standard ②        001 30  Days                    0   PC
   -> Simulation          1,00       EUR       100 PC  Net
   1619                                               5300005886
 □ 1000  Standard ③        001  5  Days                    0   PC
   -> Simulation          0,60       EUR       100 PC  Net                            X
     Pur. Order          0,80       EUR       100 PC  4500017281 00010  22.10.2015
```

Figure 4.65: Info record list displays: price simulation result

Under ❶, ❷, and ❸ you can see the price valid on **11/23/2016** for our simulation quantity of **1,000,000** pieces specified in Figure 4.64, with cash discount and delivery costs included. Because we selected the list display per vendor in our example, the cash discount proportion is the same in each case because the payment term and therefore the cash discount amount is defined in the vendor master. If you trigger the evaluation for multiple vendors with different terms of payment, the price simulation enables you to select the cheapest vendor for a material.

The delivery costs are entered in the info record under the conditions and are thus determined individually for each material. For a detailed overview of the result, click ⊞Simulation to display the following view (see Figure 4.66).

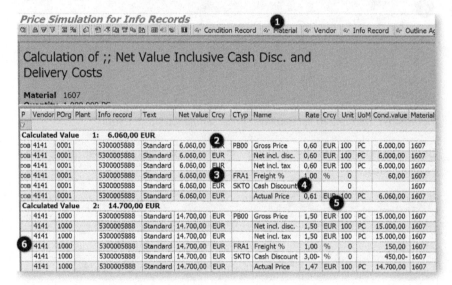

Figure 4.66: Info record list displays: price simulation details

In area ❶, you can decide whether you want to display the condition record from the info record, the material master, the vendor master record, or the entire info record for this material or vendor. To do this, position the cursor in a line to select the corresponding data.

Under ❷, you can see the gross price for this material; under ❸ and ❹ you can also see the condition records created, in this case **Cash Discount** and **Freight**. Under ❺, you can also see the actual price that you want to achieve when you create a purchase order.

The traffic light status under ❻ shows which material is the cheapest overall, taking all cost components into account. In this example, this appears trivial because there is only one material. However, as soon as you have a lot of materials with very different cost elements, this information helps you to make a decision.

Price simulation for selecting the source of supply

 With this example, I want to illustrate how the price simulation can support you in selecting the source of supply. A material **1619** can be purchased from two vendors **4141** and **4142**. The gross price for **1,000,000** pieces is identical, namely **EUR 0.30** per **100 PCS**. Nevertheless, the additional price elements produce different total costs (see Figure 4.67).

Vendor	POrg	Plnt	Info record	Text	Net Value	Crcy	CTyp	Name	Rate	Crcy	Unit	UoM	Cond.value	Material	Matl Group	Q	FixedCosts	Scale qty
alculated Value		1:	3.000,00 EUR															
4141	1000		5300005886	Standard	3.000,00	EUR	PB00	Gross Price	0,30	EUR	100	PC	3.000,00	1619		X		0
4141	1000		5300005886	Standard	3.000,00	EUR		Net incl. disc.	0,30	EUR	100	PC	3.000,00	1619		X		0
4141	1000		5300005886	Standard	3.000,00	EUR		Net incl. tax	0,30	EUR	100	PC	3.000,00	1619		X		0
4141	1000		5300005886	Standard	3.000,00	EUR	FRA1	Freight %	1,00	%	0		30,00	1619		X		0
4141	1000		5300005886	Standard	3.000,00	EUR		Actual Price	0,30	EUR	100	PC	3.030,00	1619		X		0
alculated Value		2:	2.910,00 EUR															
4142	1000		5300005889	Standard	2.910,00	EUR	PB00	Gross Price	0,30	EUR	100	PC	3.000,00	1619		X		0
4142	1000		5300005889	Standard	2.910,00	EUR		Net incl. disc.	0,30	EUR	100	PC	3.000,00	1619		X		0
4142	1000		5300005889	Standard	2.910,00	EUR		Net incl. tax	0,30	EUR	100	PC	3.000,00	1619		X		0
4142	1000		5300005889	Standard	2.910,00	EUR	SKTO	Cash Discount	3,00-	%	0		90,00-	1619		X		0
4142	1000		5300005889	Standard	2.910,00	EUR		Actual Price	0,29	EUR	100	PC	2.910,00	1619		X		0

Figure 4.67: Info record list display: example price simulation

In this example, the price difference arises due to the cash discount of 3% available from vendor 4142. For vendor 4141 we have to take 1% of freight cost into account. Therefore, the recommendation is to use vendor 4142 for this material.

137

5 Summary

With this tutorial I have given you a quick insight into one of the most important processes mapped by the SAP system. The procurement process, including the goods receipt posting and the invoice verification, can provide greater process security in a company if the opportunities offered by the SAP system are used consistently. This is important above all because especially in companies that use SAP, the purchasing volume is usually very large. This is not restricted solely to materials required for production (direct materials); it also includes all indirect materials. The costs for office materials, company cars, and business trips often amount to millions each year, for example. With these amounts, it is easy to understand that company management places great value on having a reliable and understandable process. For example, the accounts for Siemens AG for 2014 show a value of EUR 7,594,000,000 for payables for goods and services.[1]

The simple structure of the processes in Materials Management (MM) and the close integration with the Finance module make MM one of the most frequently used SAP modules.

In many large companies today, the policy is to only post and pay invoices for which a purchase order exists in the SAP system. In addition to the increased transparency, this also allows additional checks (Internal Control System [ICS] and Sarbanes-Oxley Act [SOX] for companies quoted on the stock market in the USA) to be simplified, reduced, or even avoided.

Using the following best practice tips, I would like to strongly reiterate how helpful it is to maintain data consistently in the SAP system:

▶ The entry of payment targets and Incoterms in the vendor master data ensures that the conditions negotiated by the purchasing department are applied in every purchase order.

---

[1] *https://www.siemens.com/annual/14/de/download/pdf/Siemens_JB2014_Konzernabschluss.pdf*

139

▶ A purchase requisition completed to the best possible degree makes it easier for the purchasing department to create the purchase order and accelerates the procurement process. The release process ensures that the purchase order is created based on an authorized request.

▶ Activating the order acknowledgment requirement makes everyday working life easier.

▶ A missing order acknowledgment can also be an indication that a vendor has not received a purchase order. If the SAP system sends an order acknowledgment reminder quickly, this situation is detected almost in real time—rather than only after the delivery time has passed.

▶ The goods receipt-based invoice verification ensures that invoices are only cleared once the material has been delivered or the service performed. This avoids payments to vendors or service providers if no delivery or service has been received.

▶ On the other hand, real-time posting of the goods receipt leads to faster invoice processing, cash discounts can be utilized, and there is almost no need for clarification with the vendor due to payment targets being exceeded.

Overall, I can only stress that thorough and comprehensive handling of the process ("process hygiene") means that both internal customers and external business partners are freed from unnecessary effort and expense. This leads to problem-free cooperation. The time that is saved can be used to optimize processes and enhances your own work content.

Many evaluations and documents can also be created and sent via an SAP job. This saves time and means that in the stress of your everyday work, you do not forget, for example, to regularly check the price validity. Contact your system administrator or key user in this regard. Often, the IT experts do not know the challenges presented by your daily work. However, in my experience, they are willing to help and are extremely creative in finding solutions.

I would also recommend that you take the time and effort to create key figures and evaluations yourself if you need these frequently from a colleague or another department. Many colleagues are happy for you to relieve them of some work and will gladly support you in executing the evaluation yourself. This gives you a better overview of the entire process, you avoid waiting times, and at the same time, you improve your relationship with colleagues who you would otherwise probably have to remind several times before you get the required data. The system administrator can give you the required authorizations. Getting the authorizations should not prove to be a problem because you will usually only be displaying data.

Finally, I would also like to encourage you to be open in your work with the SAP system. Try out new processes, process steps, or process variants in the test system and participate actively in designing processes in your company if you have the opportunity to do so. This can help you to expand your skills. And the more you know about the system, the less frustrated you will be if something doesn't work as you expected. You now know where to look!

I hope your first steps in the SAP module Materials Management are successful—enjoy!

Claudia Jost

ESPRESSO TUTORIALS

You have finished the book.

A The Author

Claudia Jost has been involved in process design for 15 years. During this time, she has focused on designing processes with external business partners (concentrating on procurement processes), and mapping these processes in the SAP system. Her important core tasks have also included electronic integration via EDI and optimizing internal business processes based on SAP standard applications. With regard to the design of the Electronic Manufacturing Services (EMS) process, Claudia has been responsible for integrating the entire process, from the customer order, through production, up to delivery, in SAP.

B Index

C Disclaimer

This publication contains references to the products of SAP SE.

SAP, R/3, SAP NetWeaver, Duet, PartnerEdge, ByDesign, SAP BusinessObjects Explorer, StreamWork, and other SAP products and services mentioned herein as well as their respective logos are trademarks or registered trademarks of SAP SE in Germany and other countries.

Business Objects and the Business Objects logo, BusinessObjects, Crystal Reports, Crystal Decisions, Web Intelligence, Xcelsius, and other Business Objects products and services mentioned herein as well as their respective logos are trademarks or registered trademarks of Business Objects Software Ltd. Business Objects is an SAP company.

Sybase and Adaptive Server, iAnywhere, Sybase 365, SQL Anywhere, and other Sybase products and services mentioned herein as well as their respective logos are trademarks or registered trademarks of Sybase, Inc. Sybase is an SAP company.

SAP SE is neither the author nor the publisher of this publication and is not responsible for its content. SAP Group shall not be liable for errors or omissions with respect to the materials. The only warranties for SAP Group products and services are those that are set forth in the express warranty statements accompanying such products and services, if any. Nothing herein should be construed as constituting an additional warranty.

More Espresso Tutorials Books

Björn Weber:

First Steps in the SAP® Production Processes (PP)

▶ Compact manual for discrete production in SAP

▶ Comprehensive example with numerous illustrations

▶ Master data, resource planning and production orders in context

http://5027.espresso-tutorials.com

Stephen Birchall:

Invoice Verification for SAP®

▶ Learn everything you need for invoice verification and its role in FI and MM

▶ Keep user input to a minimum and automate the process

▶ Discover best practices to configure and maximize the use of this function

http://5073.espresso-tutorials.com

Uwe Göhring:

Capacity Planning with SAP®

► How to leverage SAP Capacity Management

► Capacity planning best practices

► Options for capacity scheduling in SAP ERP

► Automatic resource and material scheduling with SAP APO

http://5080.espresso-tutorials.com

Avijt Dutta & Shreekant Shiralkar:

Demand Planning with SAP® APO—Concepts and Design

► Step-by-Step Explanations and Easy to Follow Instructions

► Combination of Theory, Business Relevance and 'How to' Approach

► APO DP Concepts and Design Explained using a Business Scenario

► Centralized Process Flow Diagram to Illustrate Integration

http://5105.espresso-tutorials.com

Avijt Dutta & Shreekant Shiralkar:

Demand Planning with SAP® APO—Execution

► Step-by-Step Explanations and Easy to Follow Instructions

► Combination of Theory, Business Relevance and 'How to' Approach

► APO DP Execution Explained using a Business Scenario

► Centralized Process Flow Diagram to Illustrate Integration

http://5106.espresso-tutorials.com

Tobias Götz, Anette Götz:

Practical Guide to SAP® Transportation Management (2nd edition)

► Supported business processes
► Best practices
► Integration aspects and architecture
► Comparison and differentiation to similar SAP components

http://5082.espresso-tutorials.com

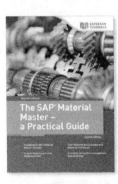

Matthew Johnson:

SAP® Material Master—A Practical Guide, 2nd extended version

► Fundamental SAP Material Master concepts
► How settings impact other modules in SAP
► Cost-effective procurement and planning techniques
► Inventory and quality management best practices

http://5190.espresso-tutorials.com

Sydnie McConnell & Martin Munzel:

First Steps in SAP® (2nd edition)

► Learn how to navigate in SAP ERP
► Learn SAP basics including transactions, organizational units, and master data
► Watch instructional videos with simple, step-by-step examples
► Get an overview of SAP products and new development trends

http://5045.espresso-tutorials.com

Made in United States
Orlando, FL
02 August 2023

35686069R00085